Diane Harris

PLANT BOWLS

COOKBOOK

Easy step by step guide for making your own Buddha bowl plant based. Hundreds of recipes with vegetarian, vegan, and gluten-free options to improve your health.

TABLE OF CONTENTS

INTRODUCTION

What is a Buddha Bowl?

Buddha bowl is a catchy name for a simple concept: a one-dish meal that's made by piling a healthy combination of whole grains, vegetables, legumes, and a luscious sauce in a large, single-serving bowl.

According to Dan Zigmond, a Zen priest and the author of Buddha's Diet, the name Buddha Bowl might have a very literal origin. "Buddha woke up before dawn every morning and carried his bowl through the roads or paths wherever he was staying. Local people would place food in the bowl as a donation, and at the end he would eat whatever he had been given. That was the original Buddha Bowl: a big bowl of whatever food villagers had available and could afford to share."

Other sources point to how the mounded top of the filled bowl looks like a Buddha statue's belly. The truth is, "bowl cuisine" as we know it has been around for decades and Buddha bowl-type meals with it. They've just been called different names—such as "grain bowls," "hippie bowls," "macro bowls," and "nourish bowls."

Tracing its origin, the concept of Buddha bowls may have originated from presenting a balanced meal, wherein balance is a key Buddhist notion.

These interesting colourful bowls make a balanced meal for breakfast, lunch or dinner. They are simple to make, beautiful to look at, nourishing and absolutely kid-friendly.

Is There A Specific Recipe?

Just as there's no one name for one-bowl meals, there's no one recipe either. They can be eaten hot or cold, made ahead or assembled at the last minute, prepared according to a recipe or thrown together with whatever's on hand. The main thing is that the bowl should have a balanced mix of ingredients that look good, taste good, and are good for you.

How to Make a Buddha Bowl

Balance is key when assembling a Buddha bowl; after that, anything goes. Buddha bowls are a well-balanced mix of protein, vegetables, and good fats that nourish you with a hearty, satisfying meal. Each bowl starts with a base typically made up of whole grains, rice, noodles, or legumes, or even a combination of those ingredients. Then it gets loaded with a generous assortment of cooked or raw vegetables, often a handful or two of fresh greens, and a boost of protein, from meat, fish, eggs, tofu, or beans, before getting finished off with a dressing, sauce, or broth. It all comes together in a big bowl, for an easy, healthy meal.

Buddha bowls are highly versatile and easy to tailor to all tastes and dietary preferences. All you need to do is just remember the formula for the bowl:

Whole grains + protein + vegetables and fruit + dressing + sprinkles = Buddha bowl

They are easy to pack and hence a great lunch box option. They offer many benefits!

Here's a quick rundown on how to make your own:

1. CHOOSE A GRAINY BASE

Fill the bottom of a large (2- to 3-cups is ideal) bowl ⅓ of the way with hot or cold whole grains, like brown rice, bulgur, barley, quinoa, or polenta. Whole grains are the most common Buddha bowl foundations, but you can also branch out to other complex carbs like potatoes, whole grain pasta, and noodles, which also absorb flavors well.

Thanks to their combination of starch (carbohydrates) and fibre, whole grains make you feel full and provide stable energy for several hours after a meal. If you have an active day in store, give yourself a boost of energy with a one-cup helping of grains. If you're planning to chill out, half a cup is enough.

2. PILE ON THE VEGGIES

You've probably heard the expression "Eat the rainbow." It's a great metaphor that makes it easy to remember that each vegetable pigment provides a unique set of health benefits. Therefore, to make the most of the rainbow's full spectrum, draw on your inner Picasso, and use a variety of colours! Aim to use about one and a half cups of vegetables overall.

Here's a bit of colour inspiration:

Green: Kale, spinach, romaine, arugula, bok choy, broccoli, asparagus, zucchini, Brussel sprouts, snow peas, sprouts, parsley, cilantro, basil...

Colourful: Beet, red cabbage, onion, carrot, tomato, cauliflower, sweet potato, winter squash, radish, eggplant, bell pepper...

Fruity: Mango, pomegranate, apple, pear, strawberry, peach, pineapple, dried fruit...

3. ADD PROTEINS

Not only is protein very effective when it comes to satiety, but the body uses protein to build and repair its various components such as muscles, skin, hair, antibodies, hormones, etc. Therefore, you'll want to include a good source of protein at every meal! From the plant world, legumes (chick peas, beans and lentils) and soy (edamame, tofu and tempeh) are also highly recommended. Add three quarters of a cup to one cup to your bowl! Fill out the bowl with ½ to 1 cup of super satiating plant-based ingredients, such as lentils, black beans.

4. HEALTHY FATS

In addition to enhancing taste, healthy fats keep the cardiovascular system happy and help the body assimilate vitamins A, D, E and K. Here a few ways to make the most of them in your meals:

- Drizzle one to two tablespoons of vinaigrette or vegetable-oil dressing (olive, canola, nut, etc.) on your bowl ingredients.
- Add creaminess with chunks of avocado, tahini or hummus.
- Sprinkle seeds over your ingredients for extra crunch (sesame, hemp, sunflower, pumpkin, flax, chia), roasted nuts (walnuts, almonds, cashews, pine, etc.) or peanuts.

5. DRIZZLE WITH SAUCE

The sauce you use to season your Buddha bowl brings together all the flavors of the base and toppings. Pestos, pasta sauces, peanut sauce, miso sauce, salad dressings, and dips all make great Buddha bowl options, and sometimes just a squeeze of lemon juice is all you need.

6. CONTRAST

Once you've met the nutritional challenge, how do you turn the basic bowls elements into a truly succulent meal? The answer is obvious: Play up the contrasts! This second principle is sure to turn your meal into a culinary success story.

Once you've met the nutritional challenge, how do you turn the basic bowls elements into a truly succulent meal? The answer is obvious: Play up the contrasts!

What do we mean by contrast? here are a few examples:

Use alternate colours: yellow, green, red, white, pink…

Include a variety of textures: creamy, firm, crispy, crunchy, soft…

Integrate different shapes: cubes, rounds, sticks, grated, julienned, whole leaves…

Play with temperature and cooking methods: raw, steamed, grilled, roasted, stewed…

Balance the flavour: sweet, salty, acid, bitter, umami.

Got A Blah Buddha Bowl? Here's How To Fix It!

Sometimes a luscious-sounding combo of your favorite ingredients ends up needing a little something to bring all those fabulous flavors together. Here are 10 quick-fix ideas to try:

- Squeeze of citrus juice

- Sprinkle of nutritional yeast

- Shake of hemp, chia, sesame, or flaxseeds

- Dash of hot sauce

- Drizzle of maple syrup

- Pinch of curry or chili powder

- Few drops of soy sauce

- Drizzle of vegetable broth

- Dollop of barbecue sauce

- Squeeze of mustard

- Swirl of tahini, tahini sauce, or nut butter.

How Long Will A Buddha Bowl Keep In The Fridge?

Since there are no highly perishable items in plant-based Buddha bowls, most of them will keep in the fridge for up to three days. Just be sure to leave off extra-juicy toppings, such as tomatoes, and fruits that may brown, such as apples and pears, until ready to serve.

Benefits of a Buddha bowl

Highly nutritious: It is packed with nutrition because of the balanced proportions of food groups in it. Further, it is antioxidant rich, because of the various coloured veggies and greens that are used. And, because very minimal cooking is involved, it conserves the loss of nutrients.

Aids weight loss: Its high fibre and protein-rich content contribute to active weight loss.

Reduces food wastage: It helps in managing food waste and leftovers, as anything available in your kitchen and refrigerator can be creatively included in a Buddha bowl.

Kid-friendly: Your little ones will be fascinated by these colourful Buddha bowls and enjoy prepping one of their very own. And, they will dig right into the bowl and eat it all up as they were involved in preparing it.

There's no perfect recipe to prepare a Buddha Bowl, and that's its speciality. Play around with different types of spices, herbs and dressing to find the combination that works best for you. Buddha bowls are mostly vegetarian and vegan and in this book we'll focus only on this kind of Buddha bowls, but you can add meat as well if you wish.

Buddha bowls tools

Okay, so you must super excited to create your first ever Buddha bowl from the recipes in this book. But before you do that, you might want to ensure that you have the tools of the trade in your kitchen.

Not to worry, for there is absolutely nothing fancy or ridiculously expensive here.

Instead, what you will need are probably already in your kitchen. We simply want you to have them all laid out neatly first so that your experience would simply "glide" through the cooking experience.

Anyway, without further ado, here are the basic kitchen tools you will need for a kitchen built for Buddha bowl building:

A bigger than average bowl

While it would be silly to prepare a Buddha bowl without an actual bowl, you might want to keep in mind that you will need a bowl with almost the same capacity as a regular plate for Buddha bowl recipes. Most bowls were designed to serve soup instead of full-blown meals, after all, and so you may want to have a relatively bigger bowl ready for serving the meals in this cookbook.

Most likely you already have a wide-mouthed bowl in your kitchen that can be perfect for your Buddha bowl. And if you do not, then you can always create "miniature" Buddha bowls for smaller, more frequent meals during the day. Whatever floats your boat, really.

Lidded bowls

Perhaps you have a stainless steel or ceramic bowl in mind for your Buddha bowl. However, you may also need to have a bowl or two that has an actual lid. That way, any excess servings you will have prepared can easily be chucked into the refrigerator for later enjoyment.

Moreover, we highly encourage you to prepare Buddha bowls ahead of time. That way, all you have to do whenever hunger pangs kick in is to grab a bowl, uncover, and dig in (unless you absolutely have to reheat it in the microwave for a few seconds first). Let's face it: chopping up veggies takes time, so meal prepping is the way to go if you want Buddha bowls to be a sustainable part of your busy life.

A good old fork (or a pair of chopsticks)

Most of the time, all you ever really need to eat from your Buddha bowl is a fork or a pair of chopsticks. The ingredients will mostly be bite-sized, so there is no need to cut anything up. Instead, you will be popping them into your mouth right away.

Now, it may take some skills to pick up the last few grains of quinoa or rice stuck in the bottom of the bowl, but you will figure it out. Besides, you can always grab the spoon and finish it up then and there.

A really sharp, reliable knife and a chopping board

Without a doubt, you will be doing loads of chopping, julienning, slicing, dicing, and mincing when you are preparing most Buddha bowls. Therefore, it helps to have a knife that can cut through anything.

With your knife, you will of course need a chopping board. Keep in mind that you should have more than one chopping board, especially if you handle meat in the kitchen. Ideally your chopping board for vegetables should be separate from the one you will use with meats.

Food Processor (sort of optional)

Aside from a knife, you might also want to invest in a food processor that can chop up things for you in a cinch. In fact, this will make life so much easier, so if you can afford it, go ahead and invest in one.

In fact, some recipes absolutely call for a food processor, especially the ones that recommend chunky to smooth sauces. Keep in mind that without this nifty modern tool, it will take you so much longer to grind up those ingredients with a mortar and pestle.

BREAKFAST

Gluten free breakfast power bowls

INGREDIENTS

- 2/3 to 1 cup cooked quinoa
- 1/4 cup to 1/3 c or less gluten free rolled oats (you can also use this as a topping

versus mix in, if you prefer).

- 2 –3 tbsp chia seed
- 8 oz coconut milk or almond milk (save extra for topping before serving)
- 1 –3 tbsp maple syrup or or honey (to taste)
- splash of lemon juice
- 1/4 tsp cinnamon
- 3 tbsp slivered or chopped nuts or seeds
- 1 tbsp cocoa nibs or dark chocolate chips
- Fruit of choice – berries, banana, kiwi fruit, etc. 1 cup or less.
- Toss fruit in a dash of lemon juice to keep fruit from browning. This is if preparing the power bowls a day ahead, for meal prep.
- Optional toppings or mix in – 1 tbsp creamy nut butter or plain yogurt to top.

INSTRUCTIONS

1. First cook your quinoa according to package instructions. Or use leftover cooked quinoa. Brown rice or millet may be substituted.

2. In a large bowl, mix together 2/3 cup to 1 cup of cooked quinoa, optional oats, and chia seed. Pour the milk on top to cover the grain/seed mix. Stir in sweetener (maple syrup or honey) and pinch of cinnamon.

3. Let this mix sit in the fridge for 30 minutes up to overnight. This mixture will thicken into a chia pudding like texture.

4. Once the grain/seed mix has thickened to your liking or you're ready to eat, remove from fridge and layer with toppings: nuts, chocolate, oats, fruit, etc. Pour a splash more of non-dairy milk or honey on top, if

desired.

5. Keeps well in fridge for up to 5 days. Makes for the perfect overnight (make ahead) breakfast bowl! You can also spoon portions into mason jars for breakfast on the go!

NOTES

- Keeps well in fridge for up to 5 days. Makes for the perfect overnight (make ahead) breakfast bowl! You can also spoon portions into mason jars for breakfast on the go!
- Nutrition below based on using almond milk (unsweetened).

Chia, Cinnamon & Apple Bircher Bowl

INGREDIENTS

- ¼ cup chia seeds
- 1 ½ cups almond milk
- 2 apples, grated
- 1 lemon, juiced
- 2 tbsp sultanas or raisins
- 1 tsp ground cinnamon

- ¼ cup crushed almonds, with some extra for serving

INSTRUCTIONS

1. Mix chia seeds and almond milk. Let sit so chia seeds can absorb the milk.
2. Grate apples and drizzle with lemon juice to prevent browning.
3. Mix apples, sultanas and cinnamon with the chia seed mix.
4. Divide between bowls, top with crushed almonds, extra cinnamon, and extra sliced apple.

Lentil Spaghetti Squash Breakfast Bowl

YIELD: 2

INGREDIENTS

- 1/3 cup lentils (I used green)
- 1 small roasted spaghetti squash*
- 1 medium sweet potato*, spiralized or diced, and cooked
- 2 eggs
- 1 small avocado
- 1/4 cup feta cheese

INSTRUCTIONS

1. Cook the lentils: Rinse lentils in fine mesh strainer. Place in small pot with 1 1/3 cups of water and bring to a boil. Reduce heat to low and simmer for about 15-20 minutes, or until tender. Remove from heat and drain excess water if necessary.

2. Add as many lentils and as much spaghetti

squash to your bowl as desired. For reference I used about 1/2 cup cooked lentils, 2/3 cup spaghetti squash, and half of the medium sweet potato for one bowl. Top with cooked egg, 1/2 avocado and 2 TBS feta.

3. Store the leftovers in fridge if necessary.

RECIPES NOTES:

*MEAL PREP TIP: You can make lentils, sweet potato, and spaghetti squash the night or couple days before. To roast spaghetti squash, cut lengthwise and rub inside with a bit of olive oil. Place face down in a shallow pan with about 1" of water and roast at 375F for about 30-40 minutes, or until tender. You don't have to use water to steam, but I've found it cooks quicker this way.

Hearty Mexican Style Breakfast Buddha Bowls

Yield: 3

INGREDIENTS

- 1 small baked sweet potato, peeled and sliced into wedges 1 small roasted poblano pepper
- 1 large avocado
- 3 hardboiled eggs, peeled

- 3 oz. sliced Monterey Jack cheese 2 garlic cloves, peeled and minced 12 oz. cooked black beans
- ¾ cup baby arugula 1/3 cup cilantro leaves
- ¼ cup crumbled feta cheese
- 1 small onion, peeled and chopped
- ¾ Tbsp. olive oil 1/3 tsp. sea salt
- 1/3 tsp. ground coriander 1/3 tsp. dried oregano 1/3 tsp. chili powder
- 1/3 tsp. ground cumin

INSTRUCTIONS

1. Place a saucepan over medium flame and heat through. Once hot, add the oil and swirl to coat. Sauté the onion until translucent, then stir in the garlic and spices. Stir until fragrant.

2. Add the beans and stir well until heated through. Cover and reduce to low flame. Simmer for about 8 minutes or until tender to a desired consistency. Adjust seasonings, if needed.

3. Divide the black beans among three bowls and then add the roasted sweet potato wedges on top.

4. Halve the hardboiled eggs and divide among the Buddha bowls. Top with the cheese.

5. Halve the avocado, remove the stone, and slice thinly. Arrange on top of the bowls. Best served right away.

Cocoa Quinoa Breakfast Bowl

Yield: 3

INGREDIENTS

- 1 banana, peeled and sliced 1 cup white quinoa
- 1 cup coconut milk 1 cup almond milk
- ½ cup mixed berries 3 Tbsp. coconut sugar 2 Tbsp. cocoa powder

- 3 Tbsp. chopped vegan dark chocolate 3 tsp. chia seeds

INSTRUCTIONS

1. Rinse the quinoa thoroughly then drain well. Set aside.
2. Place a saucepan over medium flame and heat through. Once hot, add the quinoa and stir until lightly toasted.
3. Pour the coconut and almond milk into the pot and stir well to mix with the quinoa.
4. Bring to a boil then reduce to low flame and simmer for 20 minutes, uncovered, or until the milk has been completely absorbed by the quinoa. Stir every now and then to keep the bottom from sticking to the pan.

5. Remove the pan from the heat and then stir in the cocoa powder and coconut sugar. Mix well.

6. Divide the cocoa quinoa among three bowls and top with the sliced banana, mixed berries, and dark chocolate. Sprinkle with the chia seeds and serve. May be covered, refrigerated, and served chilled.

Kedgeree

Kedgeree is a great example of an Anglo–Indian dish and it makes a brilliant one-pan breakfast. It originatedfrom the traditional Indian *khichdi*, a dish of split peas and rice but the addition of eggs and herbs such as tarragon and parsley (and flaked fish too, of course, in the more traditional version) makes clear the British influence. I love to pimp it up with some grilled halloumi, making it Anglo–Indian–Cypriot!

YIELD: 4

INGREDIENTS

1. 2 tbsp olive oil
2. 1 onion, chopped
3. 3 garlic cloves, crushed salt and black pepper
4. ¼ tsp turmeric
5. ½ tsp mild curry powder
6. 300g/10½oz/1½ cups short-grain brown rice 150g/5½oz/¾ cup red lentils 500ml/18fl oz/2 cups vegetable stock
7. 750ml/1¼ pints/3 cups water 2 stems kale, roughly shredded
8. 1 sprig tarragon, leaves plucked and roughly chopped 250g/9oz halloumi, cut

into 8 slices (optional) 4 eggs, boiled and cut into quarters

9. 3 sprigs parsley, chopped 1 lemon, cut into 4 wedges

10. 1 lemon, cut into 4 wedges

INSTRUCTIONS

1. Heat the olive oil in a large casserole dish or Dutch oven, add the onion and sauté for a couple of minutes, stirring occasionally. Add the garlic and a pinch of salt and cook for a further couple of minutes. Then stir in the turmeric and curry powder and cook for another minute or so.

2. Add the rice and lentils and pour in the vegetable stock and water, cover and cook over a medium heat for about 30 minutes, stirring

occasionally. Turn the heat down if you find it's starting to catch.

3. Remove the lid and cook over a low heat for 5–10 minutes, stirring occasionally, until the rice and lentils are fully cooked and the mixture has dried out a bit. Add the kale and tarragon and continue cooking for a couple of minutes. Season to taste with salt and pepper.

4. If using, place the halloumi slices in a hot pan or skillet and cook until golden on both sides. Remove from the pan, cut into cubes and stir them through the kedgeree.

5. Transfer to serving plates and add one egg to each portion along with some parsley and a wedge of lemon to garnish.

Alpro Fruity Breakfast Buddha Bowl

INGREDIENTS

- 10g chia seeds
- 100ml Alpro Almond Unsweetened

- 300ml Alpro Oat Unsweetened
- 100g brown rice
- 1 small avocado, peeled, stone removed, and roughly chopped
- 2 tsp cocoa powder
- 2 tsp agave or maple syrup
- 1 mango, peeled, stone removed, and chopped
- 200g mixed berries
- 2 heaped tbsp Alpro Plain No Sugars plant-based alternative to yogurt
- 20g pistachios, chopped
- flowers (optional)

INSTRUCTIONS

1. Put the chia seeds in a bowl, add the Alpro Almond Unsweetened and set aside to soak and absorb the liquid, stirring

occasionally.

2. Cook the brown rice in the Alpro Oat Unsweetened for about 30 minutes, until tender. Set aside to cool.

3. Put the avocado into a blender, along with the cocoa, agave or maple syrup and 3 tablespoons water, then blitz to a smooth purée.

4. Divide the mango and berries between two bowls, reserving some for the top. Spoon over the cooled rice, Alpro Plain No Sugars, soaked chia seeds and chocolate avocado. Scatter over the reserved berries, pistachios and flowers, if using, and serve.

Gut loving Breakfast Buddha Bowl

INGREDIENTS

- 100g coconut oil
- 150g agave or honey
- 100g organic rolled oats
- 300g mixed nuts (try polyphenol-rich;

walnuts, almonds, pecans and hazelnuts)

- 100g mixed seeds
- 1 egg white whisked (can be left out for vegans)
- 1 tbsp vanilla extract
- 1 tbsp mixed spice
- 1 tsp salt

INTRUCTIONS

1. First, preheat the oven to 100 ° c. gently melt the coconut oil in a pan with the spices and honey. remove the pan from the heat and add the vanilla extract. Once cooled slightly add the whisked egg white.
2. Combine all other ingredients in a mixing bowl and coat with the spice mixture.
3. Dish out the mixture in loose clumps onto a baking tray and then bake for around 1-

1.5 hrs until the granola mix has turned lightly golden.

4. Cool and then store in an airtight container, where the granola will keep for a couple of weeks.

CHIA PORRIDGE POTS

These delicious little pots make for a light breakfast recipe all on their own and are so simple to make. We're talking a minute or two of prep here! with goji berries long touted by the chinese as having a wide range of medicinal properties and dried cranberries, another antioxidant crammed superfood. The addition of spice to any food helps up the nutritional value tenfold and here the cardamom acts as a delicate accompaniment to the coconut milk.

INGREDIENTS

- chia seeds
- dried goji berries
- dried cranberries (no added sugar)
- 1-2 cardamom pods
- coconut milk

Simply add a ⅕ chia seeds into whatever size jar you're choosing, I'd say a mayo jar would be about right to make enough for the whole mid-week. then add in a handful or two of your dried berries and the seeds from your cardamom pods. top the rest of the jar up with your coconut milk. Give it all a good stir. And then leave it to expand overnight in the fridge. The chia porridge will last for up to about 5 days in the fridge.

SUPER GUT SUPPORTING YOGHURT

Want to know how to supercharge your yoghurt? By combining one of the most probiotic dense foods that exist in the form of kefir, packaged up neatly with its very own prebiotic gut food, Greek yoghurt. the kefir will bring the consistency of the Greek yoghurt down to that of regular yoghurt.

INGREDIENTS

- kefir
- full-fat Greek yoghurt
- separate out half of your tub of Greek yoghurt into another tub and then top both tubs up with kefir. combine the ingredients with a spoon or fork.

COMPILING YOUR BUDDHA BOWL

All that's left to do to compile your buddha bowl is to slice up some of your favourite fruit, add a scope of your chia porridge, pour on the yoghurt, sprinkle granola over the yoghurt, and then sit back and enjoy all the textures and colours of this beautiful breakfast buddha bowl that will wake your morning taste buds up with delight.

SALADES

Brazilian Salad

INGREDIENTS

- 2 carrots,julienned
- 2 small beetroots, julienned
- 45g/1½oz/½ cup shredded or desiccated coconut 60g/2oz/scant ½ cup cashews, crushed
- 40 mint leaves (30 torn, 10 chopped) 6

sprigs parsley, chopped

- 1 garlic clove, crushed 100g/3½oz/scant ½ cup natural yogurt salt and black pepper
- juice of ½ lime
- tbsp black sesame seeds

INGREDIENTS

- 4 ripe bananas
- 1 ½ cups almond water 1 cup water
- 1 cup rolled oats 6 Tbsp. chia seeds
- 1 ½ Tbsp. ground flaxseeds 3 tsp. chopped almonds
- 3 tsp. toasted coconut flakes
- ¾ tsp. ground cinnamon

INTRUCTIONS

1. Peel and mash three of the bananas in a bowl, then mix in the milk, water, cinnamon, oats, and chia seeds. Mix well and divide the mixture among three bowls.

2. Cover the bowls and refrigerate for at least 1 hour, preferably overnight.

3. Before serving, peel the last banana and then slice thinly. Arrange on top of the bowls and then top with the flaxseeds. Best served right away.

Sushi Burrito Bowl

Yield: 2 bowls

Ingredients

- 1 sweet potato, diced
- 1 tbsp. olive oil
- salt+pepper

- 1–2 large carrots, peeled
- 1/2–1 cup jasmine rice, cooked according to package directions
- 1/2 cup edamame, thawed if frozen
- 1/2 English cucumber, diced
- 1 avocado, sliced
- 1 recipe Vegan Sriracha Mayo

For serving: Roasted Seaweed (I get mine from Trader Joe's), sesame seeds, Sriracha

INSTRUCTIONS

1. Preheat the oven to 425 degrees F. Place diced sweet potato on a baking sheet. Add olive oil and salt and pepper to taste, and mix to combine. Place in the oven for 15-20 minutes, or until sweet potato is tender.

2. While the sweet potato is cooking, use a

vegetable peeler to make carrot strands. Set aside.

3. When the sweet potato is tender, assemble your bowls: Divide rice between two bowls. Top with sweet potato, edamame, cucumber, avocado, Vegan Sriracha Mayo, roasted seaweed, sesame seeds, and Sriracha (if desired).

Raw spiralized thai salad

Yield: 6

INGREDIENTS

- 1 Medium Daikon (spiralized with the C blade)

- 1 Large Cucumber (Spiralized with the C blade)

- 1 Small Green Bell Pepper (cut thin lengthwise sticks)

- 1 cup Shredded Tri-Colored Carrots

- 1 cup Sliced Bamboo Shoots

- 2 TB Raw Coconut Vinegar

- 2 TB Unsweetened Shredded Coconut

- 1/2 tsp Onion Powder

- 1/2 tsp Garlic Powder

- 1/4 tsp Coriander

- 1/2 TB Dried Cilantro

- A Dash of White Pepper

INSTRUCTIONS

1. Wash, spiralized, and prepare all your veggies. You may need to cut the daikon and cucumber spirals so they aren't too long.

2. Toss everything in a large mixing bowl. Add the vinegar, coconut, and spices. Toss to coat.

3. Place in the fridge to marinate and chill for at least an hour before serving.

LUNCH/DINNER

Roasted Cauliflower Hummus Bowls

Servings: 4

INGREDIENTS

Roasted Cauliflower

- 1 large cauliflower broken down into florets
- 2 Tablespoons extra virgin olive oil

- 1 teaspoon ground cumin

- 1/2 teaspoon chili powder

- salt and pepper

- 1/4 cup raw pumpkin seeds

Hummus

- 2 14-ounce cans chickpeas drained and rinsed

- 1/2 cup tahini paste

- 1 large lemon juiced

- 1 clove garlic

- 1/2 cup cold water

- salt and pepper

INSTRUCTIONS

1. Preheat your oven to 200°C / 400°F.

2. Spread the cauliflower florets out into a

single layer on a baking sheet. Drizzle with extra virgin olive oil, adding more as needed to make sure the cauliflower is well coated. Sprinkle with cumin, chili powder, salt, and pepper, and toss to evenly coat the cauliflower with the spices.

3. Place the cauliflower into the oven and roast for 15 minutes.

4. Remove from the oven, turn the cauliflower, and sprinkle with the pumpkin seeds.

5. Replace in the oven and roast for another 10-15 minutes, until the cauliflower is golden and the pumpkin seeds are toasted.

6. While the cauliflower is roasting, prepare the hummus.

7. Combine chickpeas, tahini, garlic, lemon juice, and salt in a food processor. Pulse a few times to break down the chickpeas.

8. With the food processor running, add the cold water in a slow stream. Stop the food processor and scrape down the sides. Taste, adjust seasonings, and add any extra water to achieve the desired consistency.

9. To serve, spoon hummus into the bottom of four bowls. Spread and swirl into an even layer. Add 1/4 of the roasted cauliflower and pumpkin seeds over the top of each bowl.

10.   Drizzle with good olive oil, sprinkle with salt and pepper. Serve with warm pita bread.

Noodle Bowl – Easy, Vegan, Gluten Free

INGREDIENTS

- 5 oz Soba/buckwheat noodles or 1/2 package
- 4 Tbsp coconut oil divided
- 3 cloves garlic minced
- 1 tsp fresh ginger grated (can substitute 1/2 tsp ginger powder)
- 1 qt. mushrooms sliced

- 1 shallot chopped

- 1.5 cup broccoli florets

- 1 carrot julienned or shredded

- 3 stalks kale de-ribbed and chopped

- green onion chopped, for garnish/topping

- sesame seeds for garnish/topping

For the Sauce

- .25 cup soy sauce

- 3 Tbsp olive oil

- 1 Tbsp lemon juice

- 2 tsp sesame oil

- 1 tbsp maple syrup (or honey, if not vegan)

- 1 tsp Sriracha or more if desired

- 1 tsp grated ginger

INSTRUCTIONS

1. Cook noodles according to package directions.

2. Whisk together ingredients for the sauce in a small bowl, and set aside.

3. Melt 2 tablespoonful coconut oil in skillet or wok, over med-high heat. Add garlic and ginger. Cook for 1 minute.

4. Add in mushrooms and cook for about 5 minutes. Remove mushrooms from skillet.

5. Melt remaining 2 tablespoons coconut oil in skillet. Add shallots and cook about 3 minutes. Add broccoli, carrots and kale. Cook about 5 minutes.

6. Add mushrooms back to skillet and cook another 3 to 5 minutes, until veggies are tender.

7. Add the cooked noodles and the sauce

to the skillet. Stir to coat. Cook about 2 minutes.

8. Serve in bowls topped with sesame seeds and green onion.

NOTES *Can use any noodle of choice, but buckwheat/soba noodles are GF; substitute tamari for soy sauce if GF.

Easy Lentil and Roasted Sweet Potato Taco Bowl

Yield: 3

- INGREDIENTS
- 1 can Simple Truth Organic Lentils {rinsed and drained}
- 2 cups sweet potatoes cubed {+ black

pepper, chili powder, turmeric, and smoked paprika}

- 1/2 tablespoon chili powder
- 1 teaspoon cumin
- 1/2 teaspoon black pepper
- 1/4 tsp sea salt
- 1/4 tsp garlic powder
- 1/8 tsp ground chipotle pepper
- 2 tbsp favorite salsa
- 2 cups organic romaine lettuce chopped
- 1/2 cup cherry tomatoes quartered
- 1 avocado sliced
- 1/4 cup shredded cheese {dairy free if necessary}
- Optional Toppings: favorite salsa sour cream {dairy-free if necessary}

INSTRUCTIONS

1. Preheat oven to 400 degrees

2. Spray baking sheet with cooking spray and spread cubed sweet potatoes into single layer. Lightly sprinkle with black pepper, chili powder, turmeric, and smoked paprika, toss to coat. Bake 10 minutes, stir and bake another 10-15 minutes or until cooked.

3. Meanwhile, add rinsed and drained lentils to saute pan with all listed seasonings {chili powder cumin, sea salt, black pepper, garlic powder, and chipotle pepper} and salsa, cook 5-7 minutes or until heated through. Stirring occasionally.

4. Once lentils are warm, taste to check seasonings and add more to your preference.

5. Once sweet potatoes and lentils have cooked, chop romaine lettuce and begin to assemble bowls. Begin by adding a layer of lettuce to the bottom of each bowl, then add half roasted sweet potatoes, half seasoned lentils, and top with cheese, sour cream, avocado and tomat

Zucchini Noodle Quinoa Bowl

INGREDIENTS

- 2 Tbsp Pine Nuts or any nut
- 2 Tbsp Raw Pepitas
- 2 Tbsp Extra Virgin Olive Oil or coconut oil
- 1/2 lb Zucchini spiralized
- 1/4 lb Beet spiralized
- 1 cup cooked Quinoa
- 1 cup Fresh Spinach
- 1/4 tsp Kosher Salt
- 1/8 tsp Black Pepper
- 1 Lemon zested and juiced

INSTRUCTIONS

1. Heat a 10" skillet over medium-high heat. Add PINE NUTS and PEPITAS; toast until fragrant and lightly browned, stirring

constantly. Transfer to a plate.

2. To the skillet, add and heat OLIVE OIL until shimmering; add ZUCCHINI NOODLES and SPIRALIZED BEETS; sauté until slightly tender, stirring as needed (1-3 minutes).

3. Add cooked QUINOA; sauté until warmed through, stirring as needed.

4. Add FRESH SPINACH LEAVES and stir until wilted. SALT and PEPPER to taste.

5. Serve warm garnished with LEMON ZEST, PINE NUTS, PUMPKIN SEEDS, and a squeeze of LEMON JUICE.

6. Refrigerate in an airtight container up to 3 days; serve chilled or reheat as desire.

Root Vegetable Power Bowl with Roasted Garlic Tahini Dressing

Servings: 2

INGREDIENTS

For the bowl

- 1 cup of uncooked brown rice – prepare according to instructions on package
- Juice from 1/2 of a lemon
- 1 large or 2 medium sweet potatoes – peeled and diced into 1 inch pieces
- 4 carrots – Peeled and cut into 1 inch pieces
- 4 parsnips – peeled and cut into 1 inch pieces
- 10 cremini mushrooms – cleaned with stems removed
- 1 15 ounce can of chickpeas – drained and rinsed well

- 6 cups of green power mix – baby spinach kale, and red swiss chard (you can use any type of greens that you like, this is what I used)
- Salt and pepper to taste

For the dressing

- 1/2 cup of tahini
- 5 roasted cloves of garlic
- 3 tablespoons of balsamic vinegar
- 1/2 cup of water
- 1 teaspoon of cumin
- 1/2 teaspoon of finely ground sea salt

INSTRUCTIONS

1. Preheat the oven to 375° and line a roasting pan with parchment paper
2. Note: Roast the garlic for the dressing

83

while you're roasting the vegetables. If you don't want to roast the whole head (click on the recipe highlighted in the post above) you can roast five peeled cloves with the vegetables.

3. Put the sweet potatoes, carrots, parsnips, and mushrooms on the baking sheet and cover with the lemon juice. Cover the pan with aluminum foil and roast for minutes. Shake the pan after 15 minutes. Uncover the pan and roast for another 15 minutes or until the edged of the vegetables are golden brown.

4. While the vegetables are roasting cook the rice according to the instructions.

5. While the rice and root vegetables are cooking sauté the power greens and chickpeas in a medium skillet with three tablespoons of water on medium heat.

Cook until the chickpeas are heated through and the greens are slightly wilted.

6. Divide the rice into two bowls and then top with equal amounts of vegetables and chickpeas. Toss with the dressing.

7. For the dressing:

8. In a blender or food processor blend the tahini, garlic, vinegar, water, cumin, and salt until smooth and creamy. Add more water if the dressing is too thick to pour. Enjoy!

Moroccan Chickpea, Quinoa, and Sweet Potato Lunch Bowls

INGREDIENTS

- 90 grams / 1/2 cup dry quinoa*
- 2 small sweet potatoes
- 150 grams / 1 cup cooked chickpeas
- 30 grams / 1 cup rucola
- Orange Ginger Vinaigrette
- 3 tablespoons olive oil
- 3 tablespoons orange juice, 1 orange
- Zest of an orange
- 1/2 teaspoon fresh grated ginger
- 1/2 teaspoon harissa, optional
- 1/4 teaspoon sea salt
- 1/4 teaspoon pepper

INSTRUCTIONS

1. Place the quinoa in a saucepan with 250 ml / 1 cup of salted water. Bring to a boil over high heat, then reduce and simmer for 10-

15 minutes, or until the water has been absorbed.

2. Cut the sweet potatoes in half lengthwise and roast cut-side down at 200C / 400F for 30-35 minutes, or until soft and browned. Cook a few extra while you're at it if you have them.

3. To assemble the bowls, divide the cooked quinoa, sweet potatoes, chickpeas, and rucola between two bowls. Top with the orange ginger vinaigrette, pomegranate arils, and pumpkin seeds. Serve warm or cold.

4. Orange Ginger Vinaigrette

5. Place all of the ingredients into a jar or bowl and mix until fully combined. Any leftover vinaigrette will keep in the fridge for up to three days.

Notes

• If you want to pack this to bring to work or school the next day, you can add the dressing the night before. If you want to keep the lunch bowl in the fridge longer than that, add the vinaigrette when you eat it.

* This is about 1 1/2 cups cooked quinoa if you've already made it.

Black Bean Buddha Bowl with Avocado Pesto

YIELD: 4

INGREDIENTS

- 1 medium head cauliflower, chopped into florets*
- 1 teaspoon paprika
- 1/2 teaspoon garlic powder
- 1/2 teaspoon onion powder

Salt and pepper

1. 1 cup farro, or other grain of choice* (gluten-free if needed)
2. 1 bunch kale, chopped
3. 1–2 cloves garlic, minced
4. 2 cups black beans, drained and rinsed
5. 1/2 cup sauerkraut
6. Sliced green onions or cilantro, for garnish

For Avocado Pesto

- 1 avocado
- 1/4 cup fresh basil, packed
- Handful of spinach (optional)
- Juice of 1/2 lemon
- 2 cloves garlic
- 2 tablespoons walnuts

INSTRUCTIONS

1. Preheat oven to 400F. Lightly grease a baking sheet.

2. Place cauliflower florets on the baking sheet. Sprinkle with paprika, garlic powder, onion powder, salt, and pepper. Stir to coat evenly. Bake for 20 minutes, until tender.

3. In a medium saucepan, cook farro (or other grain) according to package

directions. Transfer the cooked grains to a bowl.

4. In the same saucepan, heat a little water. Add kale, garlic, salt, and pepper. Cook until the kale is wilted, about 5 minutes.

5. To arrange bowls, add kale, grains, beans, cauliflower, sauerkraut, avocado pesto, and a garnish of fresh herbs.

6. For the avocado pesto: In a blender or small food processor, add avocado, basil, spinach, lemon juice, garlic, and walnuts. Pulse until smooth, adding a couple tablespoons of water if needed.

Falafel Buddha bowl

INGREDIENTS

- 3/4 cup medium bulgur
- 1/2 acorn squash , halved, seeds removed and cut into 1/2-in. slices
- 2 tbsp canola oil , divided

- 3/4 tsp salt , divided

- 12 prepared falafel

- 1/4 cup lemon juice

- 3 tbsp tahini

- 1 garlic clove , finely grated

- 2 tsp honey

- 4 cups baby arugula

- 1 medium beet, peeled and grated

- 1/4 cup pepitas

INSTRUCTIONS

1. Position racks in top and bottom thirds of oven, then preheat to 425f. set aside 2 baking sheets.

2. Bring 1 1/2 cups water to a boil in a medium saucepan. add bulgur and reduce to a simmer. cover and cook until tender, about 15 min. remove from heat and let

stand, 5 min. fluff with a fork.

3. Toss squash with 1 tbsp oil and 1/4 tsp salt, then spread in an even layer on a baking sheet. bake in top third of oven until tender and slightly browned, 10 to 12 min, turning halfway.

4. Place falafel on the other sheet. bake in bottom third of oven until hot, 8 to 10 min.

5. Whisk lemon juice, tahini, garlic, honey and remaining 1 tbsp oil and 1/2 tsp salt with 3 tbsp water in a bowl until smooth.

6. Divide bulgur among bowls, then top with arugula, beet, squash and falafel. top with pepitas and drizzle with dressing.

Buddha-Full Sunshine Bowl

YIELD: 4

INGREDIENTS

Buddha Bowl

- 1 cup brown rice
- 2 cups water
- 1 cup corn chopped
- 1 cup pineapple chopped
- 1 yellow pepper chopped
- 1/2 cup yellow cherry tomatoes halved
- 1/2 cup raw cashews chopped
- 3 tbsp hemp hearts

Dressing:

- 1/3 cup tahini
- 1/4 cup water as needed for thinning
- 1/4 cup lemon juice plus more if desired
- 1/4 tsp sea salt

INSTRUCTIONS

1. In a saucepan add your brown rice and water. Bring to a boil, then reduce to simmer and cook for 30 minutes, or as instructed on package.

2. In a bowl add cooked rice, corn, pineapple, yellow peppers, cherry tomatoes, cashews and hemp hearts.

3. Prepare your dressing by whisking together tahini, water, lemon juice and sea salt in a bowl. Drizzle over buddha bowl and toss to combine.

Hummus and Pearl Barley Bowls [Vegan]

Yield: 2

INGREDIENTS

- 1/2 medium butternut squash, peeled and sliced
- 1/2 teaspoon cumin powder
- 1 teaspoon black sesame seeds
- 1/2 teaspoon smoked paprika

- 1/2 teaspoon apple cider vinegar

- 1 can chickpeas, drained, liquid reserved

- 1/3 cup aquafaba (liquid from chickpeas)

- 1 teaspoon salt

- 2 garlic cloves, peeled

- 1 teaspoon cumin

- 1 teaspoon lemon juice

- 1 tablespoon tahini

- 1 teaspoon oil

- 1 teaspoon cumin seeds

- 2 teaspoons coriander seeds

- 1/2 cup pearl barley, uncooked

- 1/2 cup pomegranate seeds

INSTRUCTIONS

1. First, roast the squash. Preheat the oven to 390°F. Next, slice the peeled and deseed squash into 1/2-inch thick slices. Toss them in a bowl with the sesame

seeds, cumin, paprika, vinegar and a generous pinch of salt. Finally, lay them out on a tray and bake for 18-20 minutes, until fork-tender.

2. Now place the chickpeas, aquafaba, salt, garlic cloves, cumin, lemon juice and tahini in a food processor and blend until smooth and very creamy. Set this aside for now.

3. Next, place the pearl barley in a pot of boiling water and boil for 10 minutes, until cooked but still with a slight chew. Drain and set this aside.

4. Now it is time to temper the spices, heat your oil in a small saucepan over medium heat, and fry the cumin and coriander seeds for 10-20 seconds until they start to pop. Pour this out onto a plate to cool so it doesn't cook further in the pan. We

don't want burnt spices!

5. To assemble your bowls, divide the hummus between two plates and spread it out with a spoon. Lay the butternut squash slices over, and pour the cooked pearl barley over. Take the tempered spices and oil and pour this over the pearl barley. Finally, garnish with pomegranate seeds and (if you can stand it) coriander.

Yogi Bowl with Ginger Miso Tahini Dressing [Vegan]

Ayurveda explains that certain foods affect the qualities of the mind in different ways. This Yogi Bowl uses a balance of the six tastes – sweet, sour, salty, pungent, astringent and bitter – to create a simple and satiating meal, body and mind.

INGREDIENTS

For the Ginger Miso Tahini Dressing:

- 1/2 cup tahini
- 2 tablespoons white miso paste
- 2-inches fresh ginger, skin removed
- 2 cloves garlic (optional)
- 1 tablespoon tamari
- 1 lemon, juiced
- 1/2 cup water

For the Salad Bowl:

- 6 leaves kale, washed and torn
- 1 tablespoon olive oil
- 1 small sweet potato, cubed and roasted
- 1/2 cup cooked brown rice
- 1 tablespoon gomashio (a seaweed/sea

salt/sesame blend)

INSTRUCTIONS

For the Ginger Miso Tahini Dressing:

- Combine all ingredients in a high-speed blender, blend until creamy.
- Pour into an airtight container to store. Stores up to 5 days in your fridge. Makes 2 cups.

For Your Salad Bowl:

1. Preheat oven to 375°F. Wash and cut sweet potato into 1-inch cubes, toss in olive oil and sprinkle with salt.
2. Place on a baking sheet and roast at 375°F.
3. While roasting, prepare kale by washing well, removing stems and tearing leaves

into small pieces. Place in a bowl and pour 1 tablespoon olive oil on top.

4. Use your hands to massage oil into the kale leaves, making them soft and tender. If you prefer cooked kale over raw, lightly blanch the leaves in a pot of boiling water before massaging.

5. Check the sweet potato, stir to avoid sticking or burning on the pan. Once tender, remove from oven.

6. To serve, scoop 1/2 cup of warm cooked brown rice on top of the massaged kale. Top with roasted sweet potato, a healthy heaping of the tahini dressing, and a big sprinkle of the gomashio.

Note: Garlic and onions are not a part of a traditional sattvic diet, if you have too much heat (pitta) in the body or find your mind is easily aggravated by these ingredients, please exclude the garlic from the tahini dressing.

Rice And Lentil Nourish Bowl With Brussels Sprouts And Pumpkin [Vegan, Gluten-Free]

Yield: 2

INGREDIENTS

To Make the Rice and Lentil Bowl

- 1/2 cup brown lentils
- 1/2 cup basmati rice brown or white
- 3 cups water
- 1 1/2 cups Brussels sprouts

- 2 cups pumpkin, chopped into cubes

- 2 cups spinach or kale

- Sauerkraut

- Sprouts

- 1 tablespoon coconut oil for frying

- To Make the Tahini Sauce:

- 1 tablespoon tahini

- 1 tablespoon lemon juice

- 1 teaspoon gluten-free, low-sodium soy sauce

- Warm water

INSTRUCTIONS

1. Soak lentils in water at least 8 hours prior to cooking.

2. Start with roasting the pumpkin in the oven. Pre heat oven to 355°F, cook for about 30-40 minutes until nice and soft.

3. Add the lentils, rice and water to a medium saucepan and let cook for about 20-30 mins, once cooked, poor out remaining water and let sit with the lid on.

4. Cut brussels sprouts in half and cook in a frying pan for about 15 mins with coconut oil until it starts to get soft and starts to brown.

5. To make tahini sauce, mix tahini, lemon juice, soy sauce in a mug and add small amounts of warm water until it thickens. (don't add too much water or it may become too runny).

6. Get a bowl and first add in greens then rice and lentil mix, add all remaining ingredient and top with a drizzle of tahini sauce and extra lemon or soy sauce if needed.

Fall Harvest Buddha Bowl with Creamy Cashew Apple Cider Dressing

INGREDIENTS

Yield: 1

For the Buddha Bowl:

- 3 cups chopped butternut squash (about 1/2 large butternut squash)
- 3 cups chopped apples (about 2 large apples)
- 1 15.5 oz can chickpeas, drained and rinsed
- 2 tablespoons olive oil, divided
- 1 teaspoon maple syrup
- 1 teaspoon cinnamon
- 1/4 teaspoon nutmeg
- 1/2 teaspoon salt, divided
- 2 cups quinoa
- 1 small bunch kale, stems removed and roughly chopped

- 2 tablespoons pumpkin seeds (pepitas)

For the Cashew Apple Cider Dressing:

- 1 cup cashews, soaked for at least one hour
- 1 small shallot, minced (about 1 tablespoon minced)
- 1/4 cup apple cider vinegar
- 1 tablespoon dijon mustard
- 1 teaspoon honey
- 3 tablespoons olive oil
- 1/2 cup water
- 1/2 teaspoon salt

INSTRUCTIONS

1. For the Buddha Bowl:
2. Preheat oven to 400 degrees F.

3. In a large mixing bowl, toss butternut squash, apples and chickpeas with 1 tablespoon olive oil, maple syrup, cinnamon, nutmeg and 1/4 teaspoon salt.

4. Transfer to a large parchment-lined baking sheet and roast for 30-35 minutes, or until squash and apples are tender and chickpeas are crispy, tossing halfway through.

5. Cook 2 cups quinoa according to package instructions.

6. Add kale to the large mixing bowl and toss with remaining olive oil and salt. Transfer to a baking sheet and spread kale out in a single layer. Bake for 10 minutes, or until the edges of the leaves are slightly browned but still mostly green.

7. Divide quinoa evenly between bowls. Add chickpeas, squash, apples and kale. Drizzle

cashew apple cider dressing over top and sprinkle with pumpkin seeds.

8. For the Cashew Apple Cider Dressing:

9. In a high-speed blender or food processor, blend or pulse all ingredients together until smooth and creamy. Drizzle over fall harvest buddha bowls.

NOTE: If you're vegan and don't consume honey, replace with maple syrup.

Teriyaki Tofu Bowls

INGREDIENTS

Teriyaki Sauce

- 1/2 cup water
- 2+1/2 Tablespoons coconut sugar can substitute with brown sugar
- 1 Tablespoon agave nectar
- 2 Tablespoons tamari can substitute with coconut aminos or soy sauce
- 1 clove garlic minced (about 1/2 teaspoon)
- 1/2 inch fresh ginger peeled and minced (about 1/2 teaspoon). Can use 1/4 teaspoon ground ginger instead.
- 1 Tablespoon corn starch
- 2 Tablespoons water

Tofu

- 1 block extra firm tofu
- 2 teaspoons corn starch
- 1 Tablespoon tamari
- 1-2 Tablespoons neutral oil such as canola, vegetable, or grapeseed oil. This is only for pan fried method.

Bowl Ingredients

- 1 cup white rice uncooked
- 1 cup pineapple chunks
- 1 cup shelled edamame
- Toppings (all optional):
- chopped cashews
- sesame seeds
- green onions
- cilantro

INSTRUCTIONS

- Press tofu: Open tofu package and drain. Wrap with paper towels or tea towel. Sandwich in between two plates and place a heavy object on the top plate. Let sit for at least 10 minutes.

- Cook rice using your preferred method. I make mine in my Instant Pot!

Make Teriyaki Sauce

- Add all ingredients (minus 1 Tablespoon water and corn starch) to a pan over medium heat. Stir until sauce begins to thicken.

- Mix corn starch with water to make a slurry and add to sauce. Heat until thickened up. Add water to thin sauce or more corn starch 1/2 teaspoon at a time to thicken up. remove from heat.

Prepare Tofu:

- Unwrap and cut into cubes. Transfer to mixing bowl. Add corn starch and tamari. Mix well with rubber spatula.

Pan Fry Tofu (Method 1):

- Heat oil in a pan over medium heat. I will put the teriyaki sauce in a bowl and use the same pan. Cook tofu for 1-2 minutes on each side until it's a nice golden-brown color

Bake Tofu (Method 2):

- Preheat oven to 400 degrees Fahrenheit. Adjust rack to the center.
- Add tofu to parchment paper-lined baking

sheet. Bake for 20-25 minutes, flipping halfway through.

- Once tofu is cooked, mix with teriyaki sauce until evenly coated.

Assemble Bowls:

- Add cooked rice to a bowl. Top with teriyaki tofu, pineapple, and edamame. Top with desired toppings. Add an extra drizzle of teriyaki sauce!

Spicy Chipotle Buddha Bowl With Cauliflower Rice

INGREDIENTS

- 1 head cauliflower
- 1 head broccoli
- 16 ounces white mushrooms
- 3 tablespoons olive oil divided
- Garlic powder to taste
- Salt & pepper to taste
- 1 avocado sliced
- 2 scallions chopped (green parts)

SAUCE:

- 1 cup plain Greek yogurt
- 1/2 can (or to taste) chipotle chili peppers in adobo sauce
- Juice of 1/2 lime
- 3 cloves garlic minced
- Salt to taste

INSTRUCTIONS

1. Preheat oven to 450F. Move the rack to the middle.

2. Add the Greek yogurt, chilis in adobo sauce, lime juice, garlic, and salt to a blender or food processor. Blend until smooth. Pour dressing into a jar and set aside until needed.

3. Cut the broccoli into bite-size florets. Cut the mushrooms into halves or quarters, depending on size of mushrooms. Add the broccoli and mushrooms to a baking sheet and toss with 2 tablespoons of the olive oil, the garlic powder, and salt & pepper. Roast for 15-20 minutes.

4. Meanwhile, cut the cauliflower into bite-size florets. Add the cauliflower to a food processor (you may need to do more than one batch), and process on low speed

until the cauliflower resembles rice or couscous.

5. Add the cauliflower rice to a skillet with a tablespoon of olive oil and some salt to taste. Cook for 10 minutes (or until it's as tender as you like) on medium heat, covered, stirring occasionally.

6. Slice the avocado and scallions. Assemble the bowls and serve immediately.

7. Recipe Notes

8. Cauliflower rice can keep in the fridge (either cooked or uncooked) for a few days if you don't need to make all four bowls at once.

9. The spiciness of the chipotle peppers can vary. If you're sensitive when it comes to spice, I'd definitely start with less than 1/2 the can of peppers and then taste and add more as needed.

Turmeric Chickpea Buddha Bowl

Yield: 4

INGREDIENTS

For the Root vegetables

- 1 medium Beet diced into 1/4" pieces
- 1 medium Sweet Potato peeled and diced into 1/4" pieces
- 2 Tbsp Extra Virgin Olive Oil
- 1/4 tsp Kosher Salt

For the salad

- 4 cups Kale massaged with a little Olive Oil until tender
- 1 cup Uncooked Quinoa cooked and cooled
- 1 cup Turmeric Chickpeas
- 2 medium Oranges (blood orange when in

season) peeled and sliced

- 1 cup Pomegranate Arils (seeds) or fresh berries
- 1 Avocado diced
- 1 cup Sprouts or microgreens
- 1/2 cup Walnuts coarsely chopped

- For the Lemon tahini dressing
- 2 Tbsp Sesame Tahini
- 1 Tbsp Lemon Juice
- 1 Tbsp Water
- pinch Lemon Zest
- pinch Kosher Salt optional
- Make the sauteed chickpeas

INSTRUCTIONS

Roast the root vegetables

- Heat oven to 400°; toss together BEETS,

SWEET POTATO, OLIVE OIL, and SALT; place on baking sheet; bake 15 minutes, or until tender; set aside to cool.

For the salad

- Chop kale, orange, avocado, and walnuts; portion out the pomegranate, quinoa, turmeric chickpeas, and sprouts; if you're meal prepping this buddha bowl in advance, store all ingredients separately until ready to use.

Kale tip

- Add a little olive oil and salt to the kale and massage gently with your hands until kale starts to become tender. This makes it more palatable and delicious!

For the dressing

- In a small bowl, whisk together TAHINI, LEMON JUICE, WATER, LEMON ZEST, and (optional) SALT until combined; if needed, adjust the consistency by adding more tahini or water.

To serve

- Evenly divide ALL ingredients across 4 bowls and drizzle with lemon tahini dressing; serve immediately or store in airtight containers and refrigerate up to two days. If serving later, wait to add the dressing.

Buffalo Ranch Veggie Bowl

YIELD: 2

INGREDIENTS:

- 1 tablespoon sesame oil
- 1 shallot, peeled and diced
- 1/2 pint fresh crimini mushrooms, cleaned and sliced
- 1 fresh carrot, scrubbed and sliced into matchsticks
- 1/2 half avocado, peeled, pitted and cubed
- 6 Spicy Buffalo Chick-quin Wings
- 1 cup cooked quinoa
- 1 1/2 cups Ginger Lime Brussels Sprouts
- 4 tablespoons Celery Ranch Dressing

INSTRUCTIONS:

1. This recipe is really an assembly of a

couple different recipes – some prior work involved, but everything is easily finished within an hour.

2. You can cook the quinoa, use part of it to make the Chick-quin wings, and roast the Brussels sprouts at the same time. The Cool Celery Ranch comes together in minutes, and the rest of the veggies can be prepped while the Chick-quin and Brussels are in the oven!

3. In a skillet over medium heat, combine the shallot and mushrooms in sesame oil. Sauté until soft, several minutes.

4. To assemble, divide the recipe ingredient amounts into two serving bowls, drizzle the Buffalo Chick-quin with Celery Ranch Dressing.

Mediterranean Buddha Bowl

INGREDIENTS

For the roasted chickpeas:

- 1 teaspoon olive oil
- 1 can chickpeas drained, rinsed, and dried, skins discarded
- 1/4 teaspoon dried basil
- 1/4 teaspoon garlic powder
- Salt and freshly ground black pepper

For the quinoa:

- ½ cup uncooked quinoa rinsed
- 1 cup water
- For the salad:
- 2 cups mixed field greens or lettuce
- 1 cup grape tomatoes halved
- 2 cucumbers peeled, halved lengthwise and chopped
- 1 yellow bell pepper stemmed, seeded,

and chopped

- 1/2 cup pitted Kalamata olives
- 1/2 cup Homemade hummus or store-bought

INSTRUCTIONS

To roast the chickpeas

1. Move an oven rack to the middle position and preheat oven to 400 degrees. Line a baking sheet with foil or parchment paper for easy cleanup.

2. In a small bowl, combine chickpeas with olive oil, basil, garlic powder, 1/4 teaspoon salt, and 1/8 teaspoon pepper. Spread in a single layer on the prepared baking sheet.

3. Bake for 30 minutes, stirring the chickpeas and rotating the baking sheet halfway through. Remove from the oven

and cool slightly.

To make the quinoa

1. Meanwhile, combine quinoa and water in a small microwave-safe bowl. Cover; microwave for 4 minutes on high. Remove from microwave, stir, and heat again for 2 minutes longer. Stir and let stand 1 minute in the microwave.
2. To assemble the salad:
3. Layer greens in the bottom of a bowl or on a platter. Arrange the grape tomato halves, cucumbers, bell pepper, olives, chickpeas, and quinoa in sections around the bowl. Spoon the hummus in the middle of the bowl and serve.

To assemble the salad

Layer greens in the bottom of a bowl or on a

platter. Arrange the grape tomato halves, cucumbers, bell pepper, olives, chickpeas, and quinoa in sections around the bowl. Spoon the hummus in the middle of the bowl and serve

Fried 'Riced' Broccoli Bowl [Vegan, Grain-Free]

INGREDIENTS

- 1 large head of broccoli

- 1 tablespoon coconut oil

- 1 onion, sliced

- 1 teaspoon turmeric

- 2-3 garlic cloves, grated or crushed

- Pinch of unrefined sea salt and black pepper

INSTRUCTIONS

1. Cut broccoli into chunks and add it to the food processor. Pulse until broken down into rice-size pieces.

2. Melt coconut oil in a large pan over medium heat. Add the onions and sautée for about 5 minutes until they turn golden and translucent.

3. Mix in turmeric and garlic and sautée for another minute or two. Add a splash of water if the pan gets dry

4. Pour in the broccoli "rice", cover and cook for 3-4 minutes until broccoli gets tender.

5. Remove from heat, season with sea salt and pepper, and serve with other veggies and protein of choice.

Sriracha Tofu Bowl [Vegan, Gluten-Free]

Sriracha is the "red gold" of sauces. If you're a Sriracha lover like we are, you should really try this recipe; the Sriracha Tofu Bowl. Every bite is as satisfying as the last, and when your plate is empty, though your mouth may be on fire, you'll be reaching for seconds.

INGREDIENTS

- 1 can chickpeas, drained and rinsed (or 1 1/2 cups of chickpeas, if cooking your own)
- 1 tablespoon olive oil
- 1 pound red potatoes, cut into bite-sized pieces
- 1 tablespoon olive oil
- 1-2 tablespoons Sriracha
- 1 teaspoon garlic powder
- 1/2 teaspoon salt
- 1/4 teaspoon pepper
- 1 cup quinoa, rinsed
- 1 3/4 cup water
- 1 pound broccolini, washed and trimmed
- 1/2 tablespoon olive oil
- 1/2 teaspoon salt
- 1/4 teaspoon pepper

- 1/2 tablespoon sesame oil
- 1 package of Sriracha smoked tofu (or you can use regular tofu and coat it with 1 tablespoon of Sriracha)
- 1 tablespoon ginger, minced
- 2 cloves garlic, minced
- 2 tablespoons soy sauce or tamari
- 2 tablespoons rice vinegar

INSTRUCTIONS

1. Preheat the oven to 425°F.
2. Place chickpeas, 1 tablespoon olive oil, and 1-2 tablespoons Sriracha in a large mixing bowl and mix well. Transfer the mixture onto a half of the baking sheet.
3. Place the potatoes, olive oil, Sriracha, garlic powder, salt, and pepper in a large mixing bowl and mix well. Transfer the

potatoes onto the other half of the baking sheet.

4. Put the baking sheet into the oven. Bake for 30-35 minutes, turning the chickpeas and the potatoes every 10 minutes. Once chickpeas are nicely browned, and potatoes fully baked, take the baking sheet out of the oven. Set aside. While chickpeas and potatoes are baking, make quinoa as per below.

5. Place quinoa and water into a medium pot and bring to boil over medium heat. Once boiling, reduce the heat to low, cover, and simmer for 15 minutes. Remove from heat, and let sit another 5 minutes.

6. While quinoa is cooking prepare broccolini, tofu, and the sauce.

7. Place the broccolini, olive oil, salt, and pepper in a mixing bowl and mix well.

Transfer onto a baking sheet and place into the oven. Bake for 10 minutes, flipping halfway through. Once broccolini is cooked, remove from the oven, and set aside.

8. Heat the sesame oil in a pan over medium heat.

9. Once oil is hot, add tofu and fry it, turning often, until all sides of tofu are browned. Take tofu out of the pan and place on a plate covered with a paper towel.

10.   Place the ginger and garlic in the same pan that tofu was in. Cook for 1 minute.

11.   Add the soy sauce and rice vinegar to the pan and cook for another minute.

12.   Add cooked quinoa and mix it in with the sauce. Divide quinoa among 4 serving bowls. Top the quinoa with 1/4 of cooked

chickpeas, 1/4 potatoes, 1/4 broccolini, and 1/4 tofu. Serve and enjoy.

Notes

This dish can be kept in the fridge for up to 4 days. To reheat, simply place in a pan and heat over medium heat.

Sweet Potato Chickpea Buddha Bowl Gluten-Free, Vegan

Yield: 3

INGREDIENTS

- 1 can chickpeas, drained and rinsed (or 1 1/2 cups of chickpeas, if cooking your own)
- 1 tablespoon olive oil
- 1 pound red potatoes, cut into bite-sized pieces
- 1 tablespoon olive oil
- 1-2 tablespoons Sriracha
- 1 teaspoon garlic powder
- 1/2 teaspoon salt
- 1/4 teaspoon pepper
- 1 cup quinoa, rinsed
- 1 3/4 cup water
- 1 pound broccolini, washed and trimmed
- 1/2 tablespoon olive oil
- 1/2 teaspoon salt

- 1/4 teaspoon pepper

- 1/2 tablespoon sesame oil

- 1 package of Sriracha smoked tofu (or you can use regular tofu and coat it with 1 tablespoon of Sriracha)

- 1 tablespoon ginger, minced

- 2 cloves garlic, minced

- 2 tablespoons soy sauce or tamari

- 2 tablespoons rice vinegar

INSTRUCTIONS

1. Preheat the oven to 425°F.

2. Place chickpeas, 1 tablespoon olive oil, and 1-2 tablespoons Sriracha in a large mixing bowl and mix well. Transfer the mixture onto a half of the baking sheet.

3. Place the potatoes, olive oil, Sriracha, garlic powder, salt, and pepper in a large

mixing bowl and mix well. Transfer the potatoes onto the other half of the baking sheet.

4. Put the baking sheet into the oven. Bake for 30-35 minutes, turning the chickpeas and the potatoes every 10 minutes. Once chickpeas are nicely browned, and potatoes fully baked, take the baking sheet out of the oven. Set aside. While chickpeas and potatoes are baking, make quinoa as per below.

5. Place quinoa and water into a medium pot and bring to boil over medium heat. Once boiling, reduce the heat to low, cover, and simmer for 15 minutes. Remove from heat, and let sit another 5 minutes.

6. While quinoa is cooking prepare broccolini, tofu, and the sauce.

7. Place the broccolini, olive oil, salt, and

pepper in a mixing bowl and mix well. Transfer onto a baking sheet and place into the oven. Bake for 10 minutes, flipping halfway through. Once broccolini is cooked, remove from the oven, and set aside.

8. Heat the sesame oil in a pan over medium heat.

9. Once oil is hot, add tofu and fry it, turning often, until all sides of tofu are browned. Take tofu out of the pan and place on a plate covered with a paper towel.

10. Place the ginger and garlic in the same pan that tofu was in. Cook for 1 minute.

11. Add the soy sauce and rice vinegar to the pan and cook for another minute.

12. Add cooked quinoa and mix it in with the sauce. Divide quinoa among 4 serving

bowls. Top the quinoa with 1/4 of cooked chickpeas, 1/4 potatoes, 1/4 broccolini, and 1/4 tofu. Serve and enjoy.

Bali Bowls with Peanut Tofu

Yield: 4

INGREDIENTS

- 14 ounces tofu (non gmo, organic and sprouted if possible - our use firm or extra firm)
- 1 large yam or sweet potato, cut into ¾ inch cubes
- drizzle of olive oil
- 3/4 cup uncooked black rice (or other rice or grain- both optional)

Peanut Sauce Ingredients:

- 3 thin slices ginger- cut across the grain, about the size of a quarter.
- 1 fat clove garlic
- 1/4 cup peanut butter (or sub almond butter!)
- ¼ cup fresh orange juice (roughly ½ an

orange)

- 2 tablespoons soy sauce or GF Braggs Liquid Amino Acids (Note: Tamari will turn this unpleasantly dark)
- 3 tablespoons maple syrup, honey, agave or sugar substitute
- 3 tablespoons toasted sesame oil
- ½ –1 teaspoon cayenne pepper (or a squirt of sriracha sauce)
- 3/4 teaspoon salt

Bowl Veggie Options:

- 1–2 cups shredded cabbage (or use a mandolin)
- 1–2 cups shredded carrots
- 1–2 cups shredded beets
- 1 cup sliced snap peas
- ½ cup thinly sliced radishes (or

watermelon radishes)

- 1 avocado

- fresh sunflower sprouts

INSTRUCTIONS

- Preheat oven to 425 F

- Blot dry, then cut the tofu into 2 inch squares or 2-3 inch long strips (that are ¾ inch thick). Place on a parchment-lined sheet pan. Sprinkle lightly with salt.

- Cut the yam into ¾ inch cubes and place on the other side of the sheet pan (or another pan). Drizzle lightly with olive oil and sprinkle with salt. Toss and spread out.

- Make the peanut sauce, placing everything in a blender, and blend until smooth. Reserve ½ of the peanut sauce for the bowls. Use the remaining to coat the tofu. Pour over tofu and brush tops and sides and lather them up. I like to leave a very generous amount on the top of each piece. Place in the hot oven for 25-30 minutes.

- Cook the rice like you would pasta. See notes.
- Prep all your veggies. And FYI, these are just options for you, feel free to use what you like, adding or subtracting from the list.
- When the tofu is caramelized and the sweet potatoes are fork tender, assemble your bowls.
- Drizzle with the remaining peanut sauce. Or place the peanut sauce in a little dish on each bowl.

NOTES

- This would be a delicious meal prep option for healthy lunches. Totally fine served cold!

- Boil rice in 6 cups lightly salted water until tender, about 20 minutes. Drain and let stand in strainer for five minutes. Fluff with fork.

Banh mi noodle bowl

Yield: 2

Cuisine: Vietnamese

INGREDIENTS

- 2 ounces dry rice noodles
- Boiling water
- Quick pickled veggies:
- ⅓ cup rice wine vinegar
- ⅓ cup water
- 1 cup matchstick carrots (or grated)
- ½ cup sliced radishes (or try daikon or watermelon radish-like in the photos)
- 1 teaspoon sugar (or alternative equivalent, honey, maple, coconut sugar)
- ¼ teaspoon salt

Creamy Sriracha Dressing

- 4 tablespoons Vegenaise or vegan mayo (or use regular)
- 1 tablespoon water
- 1 tablespoon rice wine vinegar
- 1 tablespoon sriracha sauce (or Sambal, or Chili Garlic Sauce)
- 1 teaspoon sugar or alternative sweetener
- ¼ teaspoon salt
- 1 teaspoon soy sauce or vegan fish sauce (or regular fish sauce)

Bowl ingredients

- 6 ounces tofu, patted dry, cut into ½ inch cubes (or chicken, see notes)
- 1 cup thinly sliced cucumber
- 1 cup thinly sliced cabbage
- ½ a red bell pepper, thinly sliced
- ¼ cup fresh torn mint leaves

- ½ a jalapeno, very thinly sliced
- lime wedges
- optional additions- sprouts, avocado, daikon, grated beet, cilantro

INSTRUCTIONS

1. Cook the Noodles: Pour boiling water over rice noodles and let sit 5-6 minutes, or until softened, drain, rinse, and set aside. (I use a shallow baking dish for this).

2. Make the Pickles (don't skip!) At the same time heat ⅓ cup water and 1/3 cup vinegar on the stove in a small pot, add sugar, salt, radishes and carrots and bring to a simmer, and toss to coat well. Turn heat off. Place them in a bowl and chill (I'll put this in the fridge or freezer for few minutes)

3. Make the Creamy Sriracha Dressing: place

ingredients in a small bowl and whisk.

4. Make the Tofu Heat oil in a skillet, and season the oil with salt and pepper. Add the tofu and sear over medium heat until all sides are crispy. Stir in a little sriacha for heat at the end.

5. Prep your veggies. Slice the cucumber, bell pepper and cabbage (using a mandolin is nice, or just very thinly slice).

6. Assemble the Bowls: divide the noodles and arrange all the veggies around it. Grab the chilling pickled veggies and divide. Add the tofu to the bowls and Spoon the flavourful dressing overtop.

7. Finish the bowls with fresh mint, jalapeño slices and lime wedges.

NOTES

You could use leftover rotisserie chicken in this,

or quickly sauté cubed chicken or shrimp, seasoned with salt and pepper until golden and cooked through, then toss with a little sriacha.

Vegan green goddess bowl

Yield: 2

INGREDIENTS

- 4–6 small potatoes (purple, red or white)
- 4 radishes, sliced (or try daikon radish ribbons)
- 1 Turkish cucumber, sliced into ribbons – use a vegetable peeler
- 1 carrot, sliced into ribbons- use a veggie peeler (or try grated raw beets)
- 1 avocado, sliced in half, pixilated (or cross-hatched)
- 1 cup shelled edamame (or other beans, like green garbanzos!)
- 10 asparagus spears, or green beans!
- 10 green beans (or try snow peas!)
- Optional additions: cooked grains, butter lettuce or little gems, sunflower sprouts, pickled onions, hemp, or sunflower seeds.

Vegan Green Goddess Dressing

- one package (12.3 ounce) of silken tofu (organic, firm) like Mori-Nu Brand
- 2 fat garlic cloves
- 1 fat scallion, white and green parts
- ¾ cup-1 cup fresh herbs, packed – a combination of ¼ c Italian parsley, ¼ c dill, and 1 c tarragon is
- 3 tablespoons olive oil
- 1 tablespoon lemon, more to taste
- 1 tablespoon vinegar – white, sherry, apple cider or champagne
- 1 tablespoon water, more to get blender started
- 1 teaspoon kosher salt
- 1 teaspoon white miso paste- optional but adds depth!

- ½ teaspoon pepper

INSTRUCTIONS

- Bring a medium pot of salted water to simmer on the stove and add the potatoes, whole. Cover and simmer gently until fork tender, about 15 minutes. (You will reuse this water for blanching the other veggies- so don't dump it out).
- Prep the radishes, cucumber, carrot ribbons and avocado, and make the dressing.
- Using a slotted spoon, remove the potatoes and set aside, saving the warm water. Drop the edamame, asparagus, and green beans into the same hot water and simmer for just a few minutes until

everything is tender and bright green. Strain.

- You can chill everything and serve over a bed of tender spring greens and grains, or you can serve this warm or at room temperature, over warm grains.
- Divide between two bowls and serve with dressing.

VEGAN Green Goddess Dressing

- Place all ingredients in a blender. Blend until smooth, adding up to one more tablespoon water, if necessary, to get the blender going. Scrape down sides, blend again. Taste, adjust salt and lemon.
- Makes 1 ¾ cups dressing and this will keep up to 7 days in the fridge.

Zen noodle bowl

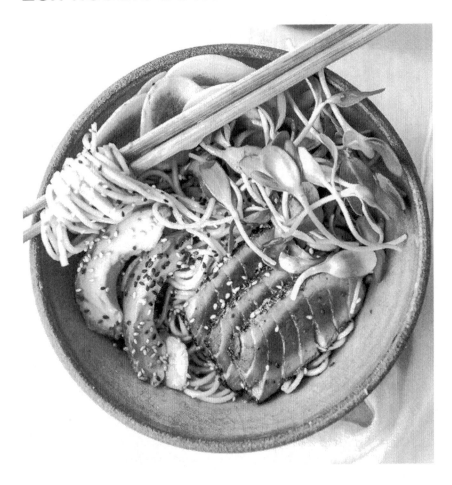

Yield: 2

Cuisine: Japanese

Vegan and Grain-free adaptable!

INGREDIENTS

- 4 ounces dry soba noodles (or rice, rice noodles, GF noodles, or cooked zucchini noodles)
- 6 ounces ahi tuna or tofu (see notes)
- 1–2 tablespoons coconut or high temp cooking oil
- 2 radishes (watermelon radishes are pretty)
- 1 Turkish cucumber, sliced (or carrot, shredded)
- ½ avocado, sliced
- garnish- scallions, chives, chive blossoms
- handful sprouts- sunflower or daikon are nice

173

- other options: grated veggies like carrots, cabbage, kohlrabi, beets, snow or snap peas, edamame, fresh peas, daikon, baby spinach or greens.

Sesame crust

- 2 teaspoons sesame seeds
- ½ teaspoon kosher salt
- ½ teaspoon granulated onion or garlic
- ¼ teaspoon sugar (optional, helps caramelize)
- ¼ teaspoon chili flakes

Ponzu Dressing:

- ¼ cup orange juice (juice from ½ an orange)
- ⅛ cup soy sauce or GF Liquid Aminos or coconut aminos (smoked shoyu is nice too).

- ¼ cup mirin (or sub a mix of 2 teaspoons honey and 3 tablespoons water)
- 1 tablespoon rice wine vinegar
- ⅛ cup toasted sesame oil
- ¼ teaspoon hondashi granules (optional- adds a nice smoky depth, but not vegan)
- pinch salt and pepper

INSTRUCTIONS

1. Cook noodles according to directions, drain and set aside.
2. While noodles are cooking, pat dry tuna. Mix the Sesame Crust ingredients together on a small plate and coat all sides of tuna, pressing it firmly into the flesh. See notes for tofu.
3. Make the dressing, set aside.
4. Heat the oil in a cast iron skillet until

smoking hot. You want the pan to be very hot- in order to create the golden crust, without cooking the ahi all the way through. Sear all sides of the tuna for 45-60 seconds on each side, or until the crust is golden. Remove from heat and place on paper towel. Let stand 5 minutes. With a sharp chefs knife, slice across grain into 6-8 thin pieces. The goal is to have the inside nice and rare and but the outside seared and crispy. The secret is the very hot pan.

5. Divide the noodles among two bowls. Divide the ahi, cucumber, radishes, avocado and sprouts among the two bowls. Sprinkle veggies and noodles with a little salt. Top with scallions or chives or chive blossoms.

6. Spoon a generous amount of Ponzu dressing over top and serve (you most

likely won't need all the dressing).

Notes

If keeping this vegan, serve it up with Sesame Ginger Baked Tofu or simple pan-seared tofu, seasoned with salt and pepper.

Spicy mexican oaxacan bowl

Yield: 2

Cuisine: Mexican Bowl

Category: Vegan Main

INGREDIENTS

Spice Rub

- 2 teaspoons cumin
- 1 teaspoon ground chipotle (or swap out a mix of smoked paprika and chili powder)
- ½ teaspoon kosher salt

Sheet Pan ingredients

- ½ a red onion, cut in ½ inch wedges
- 1 medium yam or sweet potato- diced into ¾ inch cubes (leave skin on)
- 8 baby bell peppers, cut in half (or 1

regular red or yellow bell pepper, cut into strips)

- ½ cup pecans
- 2 teaspoons maple syrup
- 15-16 ounce can Seasoned Black Beans (Cuban style or Mexican style) or use regular black beans (see notes)

Garnish: Avocado, cilantro, scallions, Cabbage Slaw, Mexican Secret Sauce or Vegan Avocado Sauce

Quick Cabbage Slaw

- ¼ of a red cabbage, shredded
- tablespoon olive oil
- ¼ cup chopped cilantro or scallions or both
- 1 teaspoon coriander

- 1/8 teaspoon kosher salt
- 1 tablespoon lime juice

INSTRUCTIONS

1. Preheat oven to 400F
2. Mix cumin, chipotle and salt together in a small bowl.
3. Place onion, sweet potato and peppers on a parchment lined sheet pan. Drizzle onion and potato with a little olive oil and sprinkle generously with spice mix, tossing to coat all sides well. Use about ½ or ⅔ of the spice.
4. Place in the oven for 20-30 minutes, tossing halfway through.
5. On another smaller parchment-lined pan, toss the pecans with 2 teaspoons maple syrup and 1 teaspoon of the spice mix.

Place in the oven (on a lower rack) for 10-12 minutes, or until lightly browned. When you pull it out, give nuts a quick toss to loosen them up and "fluffen" them, so when they cool, they are easy to remove.

6. Heat the seasoned beans in a small pot on the stove (see notes) and make the slaw. Finely chop or shred the cabbage and place in a medium bowl with the rest of the ingredients, toss. Taste, adjust lime and salt.

7. Slice the avocado.

8. When the veggies are fork tender, assemble the bowls. Divide the beans among 2-3 bowls. Divide all the veggies, placing them over the beans, and top with slaw and add the avocado.

9. Serve with the Chipotle Mayo (vegan-adaptable) or Vegan Avocado sauce if you

like, or sour cream and hot sauce– it's fine without though too.

NOTES

If using unseasoned black beans, drain and jazz them up with ⅛ teaspoon salt, ½ teaspoon cumin and ½ teaspoon chili powder. You could also add sautéed onion and garlic, and canned green chilies, or canned chipotles (the adobo sauce from the can is especially nice.) If using seasoned black beans, no need to drain.

Seoul bowl (vegan bibimbap!)

Vegan

Yield: 3

Cuisine: Korean

INGREDIENTS

- 2 cups cooked rice- short grain brown is my preference
- batch Korean Baked Tempeh (meat-eaters see notes)
- 1 cup steamed, grated or matchstick carrots (or keep fresh)
- handfuls steamed spinach (or keep fresh)
- ounces steamed shiitake mushrooms
- 1 turkish cucumber, cut into thin disks
- generous pinch salt and splash rice wine vinegar
- ⅛ cup thinly sliced red onion (optional)
- ½ cup fresh kimchi

185

- Garnishes – scallions, cilantro, chili paste, sesame seeds, soft boiled eggs

Korean Baked Tempeh:

8 ounce package tempeh

Tempeh Marinade:

- ½–2 tablespoons korean chili paste (Gochujang) – or use chili garlic paste or sriracha sauce
- 1 tablespoons sesame oil
- tablespoons maple syrup or brown sugar
- 1 ½ tablespoons soy sauce or GF alternative
- 1 teaspoon rice wine vinegar

Seoul Sauce: (The Dressing)

- tablespoon soy sauce or GF alternative,
- 1 tablespoon sriracha, or Gochujang
- 1 tablespoon sesame oil

- 1 tablespoon maple syrup

INSTRUCTIONS

- Preheat oven to 400F
- Set rice to cook and start the tempeh. Simmer the block of tempeh in a medium pot, with 2 inches of boiling water for 6-8 minutes to remove bitterness.
- Whisk marinade ingredients together in a small bowl, and at the same time whisk Seoul Sauce ingredients together in another separate small bowl.
- Remove tempeh from water carefully and pat dry. Cut in half, then cut in half to make thin pieces. See photos. Cut into squares, then triangles or strips. Dip each piece in the marinade and place on a parchment– lined sheet-pan, spooning

any remaining marinade over top, and bake for 20 minutes, or until crispy.

- While the tempeh bakes, prep your veggies and garnishes.
- Soft boil your eggs if using.
- Cut the cucumber, place in a small bowl and season with generous pinch salt, a splash of rice vinegar, optional red onion and sesame seeds.
- In a medium sauce pan, bring ½-1 inch of water to a simmer. Add the carrots and gently steam, just until wilted, about 2 minutes. Using a slotted spoon remove, and place on a large plate. To the same simmering water, add the spinach, steam just until lightly wilted (1-2 minutes) remove, drain, place on the same plate next to the carrots. Remove and discard the shiitake stems and place the

mushroom caps in the same simmering water, turning to steam both sides. Add little more water if you need to. Once tender, about 4 minutes later, place them on the plate next to the carrots and spinach.

- Prep any garnishes you plan to use- cut scallions, tear cilantro leaves, and gather the kimchi, sesame seeds and hot chili paste – getting the bowls ready to assemble.

- Once the rice and tempeh are done, assemble the bowls.

- Divide the rice and tempeh into 2 extra hearty bowls or 3 medium bowls. Surround with the wilted veggies, cucumbers, kimchi, optional egg, fresh herbs and sprinkle with sesame seeds.

- Spoon the flavorful Seoul Sauce over top.

189

- Eat with chop sticks and enjoy!

NOTES

- If you don't want to use tempeh, feel free to sub tofu, salmon or chicken using the same marinade. You may need to adjust the cooking time. If you have a beef lover amongst you, Traders Joe's Bulgogi Beef is a nice option, especially when grilled. You can cook both tempeh and meat (like chicken for example) on the same sheet pan, in separate corners for more options if you have vegans and meat eaters in the same house. Very adaptable!

Superfood walnut pesto noodles!

Yield: 1

Vegan and GF adaptable!

Cuisine: Northwest

INGREDIENTS

Super Food Walnut Pesto Recipe: (4-6 servings)

- cup walnuts

- tablespoons sesame oil (or olive oil)

- tablespoons white miso

- 1–2 garlic cloves, start with one

- ¼ cup water

- 3–4 cups baby superfood greens (baby kale, arugula, spinach, chard)

- squeeze of lemon to taste

Bento Box: (2 servings)

- 4 ounces dry soba noodles (sub GF noodles)

- ½ cup shredded cabbage

192

- ¼ cup sliced radishes

- cup of power greens

- ⅛– ¼ cup walnuts

- olive oil and lemon for drizzling

- optional additions: edamame, sunflower sprouts, avocado, snow peas

INSTRUCTIONS

1. Begin by getting your soba noodles cooking, cook according to directions.

2. Make the Superfood Walnut Pesto: Place walnuts, miso, oil, garlic and water into a food processor and pulse repeatedly. Add the power greens and pulse. Adjust consistency by adding more water if you like. Add a squeeze of lemon, pulse, and taste. Add more garlic, lemon or salt to taste. (The miso is satisfyingly salty so I

didn't add salt.)

3. Toss the noodles with ⅓-½ of the walnut pesto (you will have enough walnut pesto for 4-6 servings).

4. Place noodles in a bento box with a handful of greens, shredded cabbage, walnuts and radishes. (Feel free to add avocado, or other veggies) Drizzle veggies with a little olive oil, lemon and salt. Pack it up with a set of chopsticks and you are good to go.

NOTES

Superfood Walnut Pesto keeps for 5 days in the fridge.

Sunshine bowl w/ sunflower seed tahini sauce

Vegan and GF!

Yield: 4

Cuisine: Vegan

INGREDIENTS

- 4 cups hot cooked brown rice, quinoa or other whole grain
- cup cubed extra-firm tofu
- 4 Cups fresh raw crunchy veggies, grated and/or sliced – grated beets, grated carrots, radish, daikon, kohlrabi, cucumber, jicama, peppers, tomatoes
- cups packed leafy green–kale, spinach or arugula
- T chives or scallions- chopped
- 2 T sunflower seeds
- tsp Braggs Liquid Aminos (or tamari or

soy sauce)

Sunflower Seed Tahini Sauce

- ¼ cup sunflower seeds – roasted or raw
- ¼ cup fresh orange juice (half an orange)
- 2 tablespoons nutritional yeast flakes
- 2 tablespoons Bragg's Liquid Amino's or soy sauce
- 2 tablespoons apple cider vinegar
- ½ cup water
- 1–2 cloves garlic
- tablespoon fresh ginger (optional)
- tsp toasted sesame oil
- 1 tsp bee pollen (optional)

INSTRUCTIONS

- Cook grain or rice according to directions. Drizzle 1 teaspoon Braggs liquid amino

197

over cubed tofu in a bowl and set aside, letting it marinate.

- Prep all veggies (peel- then grate or slice).

- Make sunflower tahini sauce– place all ingredients in a blender and blend until smooth.

- When grain is cooked, divide among 4 bowls. Top with chopped kale. Arrange veggies and tofu overtop.

- Drizzle with tahini sauce. Garnish with chopped chives (or scallions) and sunflower seeds.

- Notes: you can also pan sear tofu (blot dry after marinating and coat in cornstarch, sear in oil until crispy)

Summer Buddha Bowl

INGREDIENTS

Rice and veggies

- ¼ cups short-grain brown rice or long-grain brown rice, rinsed
- ½ cups frozen shelled edamame, preferably organic
- 1 ½ cups trimmed and roughly chopped snap peas or snow peas, or thinly sliced broccoli florets
- 1 to 2 tablespoons reduced-sodium tamari or soy sauce, to taste
- 4 cups chopped red cabbage or spinach or romaine lettuce or kale (ribs removed)
- ripe avocados, halved, pitted and thinly sliced into long strips (wait to slice just before serving, see details in step 5)
- Essential garnishes

- 1 small cucumber, very thinly sliced

Carrot ginger dressing*

- Thinly sliced green onion (about ½ small bunch)
- Lime wedges
- Toasted sesame oil, for drizzling
- Sesame seeds
- Flaky sea salt

INSTRUCTIONS

1. Bring a large pot of water to boil (ideally about 4 quarts water). Once the water is boiling, add the rice and continue boiling for 25 minutes. Add the edamame and cook for 3 more minutes (it's ok if the water doesn't reach a rapid boil again). Then add the snap peas and cook for 2

more minutes.

2. Drain well and return the rice and veggies to the pot. Season to taste with 1 to 2 tablespoons of tamari or soy sauce and stir to combine.

3. Divide the rice/veggie mixture and raw veggies into 4 bowls. Arrange cucumber slices along the edge of the bowl (see photos). Drizzle lightly with carrot ginger dressing and top with sliced green onion. Place a lime wedge or 2 in each bowl.

4. When you're ready to serve, divide the avocado into the bowls. Lightly drizzle sesame oil over the avocado, followed by a generous sprinkle of sesame seeds and flaky sea salt. Serve promptly.

5. If you intend to have leftovers, wait to complete step 4 just before serving (otherwise the avocado will brown too

soon). Leftover bowls keep well (avocado excluded) for 4 to 5 days in the refrigerator.

NOTES

- *CARROT GINGER DRESSING NOTE: You're probably only going to need ½ batch of the dressing for 4 bowls. I recommend making the full batch since blenders require a decent volume of liquid to blend. Just use the leftover dressing on salads within 1 to 2 weeks of making.
- *MAKE IT QUICK: If you're in a hurry, you can skip the dressing and drizzle tamari and toasted sesame oil lightly over the bowls instead.
- MAKE IT VEGAN: Be sure to follow the vegan option while making the carrot-

ginger dressing.

- MAKE IT GLUTEN FREE: Be sure to use certified gluten-free tamari, instead of soy sauce. Or, omit the soy sauce altogether and season the rice with salt, to taste.

- MAKE IT SOY FREE: Omit the tamari/soy sauce and season the rice with salt, to taste.

- RECOMMENDED EQUIPMENT: I love my Vitamix blender for making the dressing and this colander for draining the rice and veggies (those are affiliate links).

Buddha Bowl with green tahini sauce

Yield: 2

Vegan and gluten-free.

INGREDIENTS

FOR THE BUDDHA BOWL:

- 1–2 Tablespoons extra-virgin olive oil
- ½ pound (225g) small yukon potatoes, halved
- 15-ounce can (425g) chickpeas, drained and dried
- 1 teaspoon ground paprika
- ½ teaspoon chili powder
- 1 avocado, halved and sliced
- 1 cup (100g) red cabbage, shredded
- 1 cup (225g) fresh baby spinach
- 2–3 Tablespoons seeds (pumpkin, sunflower, sesame...)
- Bonus ingredient: 1 cup uncooked

quinoa*

FOR THE GREEN TAHINI SAUCE:

- ¼ cup (65g) tahini
- 2 Tablespoons water, or more as needed
- Tablespoon fresh lemon juice
- ½ cup chopped cilantro or basil leaves
- ¼ small shallot, minced
- Salt and pepper, to taste

INSTRUCTIONS

1. Heat olive oil in a large skillet over medium-low heat. Add halved potatoes and cook until softened, 8 to 10 minutes, stirring from time to time.

2. Add drained and dried chickpeas and cook for 2 additional minutes, shaking the pan regularly. Stir in half of the paprika, half of

the chili powder and a pinch of salt.

3. Meanwhile, prepare the green tahini sauce in a food processor or blender by mixing all the ingredients together, until desired consistency (feel free to add more water as you go if the dressing is too thick). Taste and adjust seasoning as needed.

4. Assemble the buddha bowls* dividing in each bowl the roasted halved potatoes, chickpeas, red cabbage, avocado halves, and spinach. Sprinkle with seeds all over and serve along with the green tahini sauce. Enjoy!

NOTES

o Unlike most buddha bowls, this recipe doesn't call for quinoa as I find it very satisfying the way it is. That being said, you can totally add a portion of quinoa if you wish. Just use 1 cup (180g) uncooked quinoa and cook according package instructions before adding to the bottom of the bowl.

Lemon Basil Buddha Bowls With Lemon Tahini

Cuisine: Vegan, Gluten-Free, Oil-Free

Yield: 2

INGREDIENTS

LEMON BASIL BUDDHA BOWLS

- sweet potato, scrubbed and cut into "fries"
- 2 cups kale, chopped
- bunch asparagus, washed and woody stems removed
- 1/4 tsp garlic
- 1/2 tsp dried basil
- juice from 1/2 lemon
- 1/2 cup steamed edamame
- cup cooked toasted quinoa

LEMON TAHINI DRESSING

- 1/4 cup runny tahini
- 1/4 cup water + more as needed to thin
- 1/4 cup lemon juice
- Himalayan sea salt
- Black pepper

- FOR SERVING:
- fresh basil
- crushed red pepper
- squeezed lemon
- hemp hearts
- sprouts

INSTRUCTIONS

1. Preheat oven to 400°F and line a baking sheet with parchment paper.
2. Slice your sweet potato into thick "fries" and arrange on the parchment covered

baking sheet so they aren't touching.

3. Squeeze lemon juice all over the "fries" and sprinkle them generously with dried basil.

4. Bake for 25- 30 minutes, or until golden brown and lightly crispy around the edges. Bake longer to achieve crisper, if desired.

5. While the sweet potatoes are baking, prepare your quinoa if you haven't already done so by following packaging instructions.

6. Steam asparagus and frozen edamame on the stovetop until bright green and tender crisp (only about 3-4 minutes!)

7. To make the lemon tahini dressing, add all ingredients to a bowl and whisk to combine, adding more water as needed to achieve desired consistency.

8. To assemble, divide kale and quinoa between two bowls and top with steamed asparagus, lemon basil sweet potato fries, and edamame.

9. Drizzle with lemon tahini dressing and serve with optional sprouts, fresh basil, lemon, crushed red pepper, and hemp hearts.

10. Store leftovers separately in the fridge for 3-5 days and reheat before serving.

Macro Bowl With Carrot-Ginger-Almond Sauce

INGREDIENTS

Carrot-Ginger-Almond Sauce

- C Chopped carrots/2 medium/ approox 135g
- 1 " Fresh ginger, minced
- 1 small clove of garlic
- 1/2 Tbsp White miso
- 1/2 Tbsp Maple syrup
- 1/2 Tbsp Tamari
- Tbsp Almond butter
- 1/4 tsp Ground turmeric
- 1 Tbsp Water

Macro bowl

- 1/3 C Brown rice
- head Pak Choi, roughly chopped
- 1/2 C Cooked adzuki beans

- Tamari
- Seaweed sprinkles OR Rehydrated sea vegetables (e.g. dulse or wakame)
- Toasted sesame seeds

INSTRUCTIONS

For the sauce:

- Steam the carrots until tender then blend all ingredients together until smooth. I use my Tribest personal blender.
- Cook the rice, according to package instructions.
- Warm through the beans in a pan with a litle water. Season with splash of tamari
- Steam the pak choi for a couple of minutes, until just tender.
- Add the rice, beans and pak choi to a bowl, top with a generous spoonful of the

sauce and sprinkle with seaweed and toasted sesame seeds.

Bowl With Turmeric-Tahini Dressing

Yield: 2

INGREDIENTS

- pickled red cabbage
- 1/2 head red cabbage sliced very thinly (use a mandoline if you have one)
- cup apple cider vinegar
- 1 cup water
- 1 tablespoon agave syrup
- 1 teaspoon salt

TURMERIC-TAHINI SAUCE

- 1/4 cup tahini
- 1/4 cup water
- 1/4 cup lemon juice
- tablespoon maple syrup
- 1 1/2 teaspoons liquid aminos

- 1/2 teaspoon turmeric
- 1/4 teaspoon ground ginger

MACRO BOWL

- 2 medium sweet potatoes, peeled and sliced into coins or cubed
- olive oil spray
- salt and pepper to taste
- bunch of kale, de-stemmed and roughly chopped
- 1/2 cup dried wakame, soaked (rehydrated) in water for 5 minutes
- cups cooked brown rice (or grain of choice)
- cups (or one 15-ounce can, rinsed and drained) cooked chickpeas (or legume of choice)
- 1/2 English cucumber, spiralized into noodles or chopped

- 1/2 avocado, sliced
- sesame seeds for sprinkling

INSTRUCTIONS

1. Make the pickled red cabbage at least 3 to 4 hours prior to serving the bowl (a day in advance would be preferable). place the red cabbage in a large jar or airtight container. in a large measuring cup, combine the apple cider vinegar, water, agave syrup, and salt. pour the liquid over the red cabbage and press the cabbage down so that it is fully covered. cover the jar/container and place in the refrigerator until ready to serve (again- this should be at least 3 to 4 hours prior).

2. To make the turmeric-tahini dressing,

combine the dressing ingredients in a cup or small bowl and whisk until combined. chill until ready to use.

3. Preheat the oven to 425 f. line a baking sheet with parchment paper. spread the sweet potatoes out on the sheet. spray with olive oil and sprinkle salt and pepper. toss until fully coated. roast in the oven for 20 to 25 minutes or until easily pierced with a fork, flipping once halfway through to ensure even cooking.

4. Fill a large shallow sauce pan or medium pot with about 1 to 2 inches of water. place a steamer basket in the pot and fill the basket with the chopped kale. cover the pot and turn the heat up to hi. Once the water begins to boil, or after about 4 to 5 minutes, remove the kale from the basket and combine in a bowl with the

rehydrated wakame.

5. In 2 serving bowls, divide the cooked grains, legumes, cucumber, and sweet potato. add a generous serving of the kale and wakame mixture and top with slices of avocado and a generous serving of pickled red cabbage. Drizzle the dressing over the top (and keep it handy in case you want to add more as you eat it) and then sprinkle the bowls with sesame seeds. serve and enjoy!

NOTES

- Sauerkraut or any other pickled/fermented veggie can be used in place of the pickled RED CABBAGE.
- To make these bowls to go, prepare the

bowls in airtight containers up until the point of adding the dressing (though you can add the sesame seeds). Pack the dressing separately. Chill both until ready to eat.

Spring Macro Bowl

Yield: 3-4

INGREDIENTS

- 1/2 cups cooked white quinoa
- 6 cups kale, massaged
- 1 bunch of asparagus
- 1 can chickpeas, drained and rinsed
- 1/2 cup cooked green peas
- 4 artichoke hearts, sliced
- 3–4 radishes, sliced
- 1/4 cup chopped pistachios
- kale pesto hummus
- handful of mint leaves
- 1 TBSP hemp hearts
- sliced avocado, optional

INSTRUCTIONS

1. If you haven't already cooked your quinoa, prepare it first according to package instructions.

2. Rinse the asparagus and snap off the woody ends. Steam them in a pan on the stove top with peas for 2-3 minutes, until vibrant green and fork tender.

3. While quinoa is cooking, prepare your bowl additions for serving.

4. Chop the pistachios, slice the artichoke heats, slice the avocado and radish, and rinse the kale and mint leaves.

5. Massage the kale with lemon juice and allow to sit and wilt slightly.

6. To assemble the bowls, divide kale and quinoa between bowls and top with

chickpeas, peas, artichoke hearts, pistachios, avocado, and sliced radish. Add a dollop of kale pesto hummus and garnish with mint leaves and hemp hearts.

7. Store leftovers separately in the fridge and throw together for easy leftover lunches.

DESSERT

Chia Pudding Bowl with Coconut Milk and Berries

INGREDIENTS

- cup unsweetened coconut milk (the lower-fat refrigerated kind, such as Silk – not canned)
- 1/4 cup chia seeds
- 1 tablespoon pure maple syrup
- 1 tablespoon sugar
- 1/2 teaspoon vanilla
- 1/4 cup blackberry jelly or preserves (preferably 100% pure fruit, such as Smucker's Simply Fruit)
- 1 cup fruit (blueberries, sliced strawberries and sliced bananas – see note)
- 1/4 cup granola (such as Cascadian Farm Oats & Honey)

INSTRUCTIONS

- Mix coconut milk, chia seeds, maple syrup,

232

sugar, and vanilla in a medium bowl with a spoon or whisk, stirring thoroughly to combine.

- Set aside briefly and stir or whisk again after about 10-15 minutes to break up any clumps of chia seeds.

- Cover with plastic wrap and refrigerate at least an hour or two, or overnight. At this point, you can divide it into 4 single-serve containers such as the adorable Weck jars we used in our photos, or leave your pudding in a large serving bowl to portion out later. The pudding will be soft-set after about 1 hour. But, if possible, we recommend waiting at least 2 hours before eating, until the pudding is creamier and more fully set.

- When ready to serve the pudding, if it's not already divided into single-serve containers, portion out 4 equal servings. Top each serving with 1 tablespoon jelly, 1/4 cup fruit (or a little more, if desired) and 1 tablespoon granola. Serve immediately.

NOTES

1. Fruit topping: We specify a combination of blueberries, strawberries and bananas, since that's what First Watch uses in their "original" version. But feel free to swap in other berries, too, such as blackberries or raspberries. And don't obsess about using exactly 1/4 cup for each serving – that's just a starting point for you. Feel free to pile on more delicious, healthy berries if you'd like!

2. Thickness and consistency: As we discuss in greater detail in the post, we've extensively tested the proportion of chia to coconut milk in this recipe, to find the thickness and texture we prefer. But, you can adjust that to your own preferences by slightly varying the amount of chia and/or coconut milk. For example, a ratio with slightly less milk (or more chia) will yield a thicker pudding.

3. Make-ahead and meal prep: The base for this Chia Pudding keeps well, covered in the refrigerator, for at least 3-5 days. You might want to make a double batch for quick, grab-and-go breakfasts (and even snacks) all week long. We recommend waiting to add the toppings until just before serving, however, so the fruit is really fresh and the granola is crunchy.

Dessert buddha bowl

INGREDIENTS

- Sweet potato noodles
- ~1 cup sweet potato noodles
- tsp coconut oil
- ½ tsp coconut sugar
- ¼ tsp Ceylon cinnamon

Other toppings

- tiny avocado hearts
- berries
- fresh mint leaves
- coconut whip + a pinch of beetroot powder (just for the color if you wish)

INSTRUCTIONS

- Sweet treats like my Strawberry cheesecake bites and chocolate chip cookies.

- Instructions

- Make sweet potato noodles. Warm up coconut oil in a pan, add noodles, cinnamon and sugar. Pan fry noodles for about 5-10 minutes until they are softer with a little bit of crunch left.

- Assemble your dessert buddha bowl by adding all your favorite treats, sweet potato noodles, berries and coconut whip to the bowl.

Enjoy your dream dessert!

Blueberry Banana Smoothie Bowl

Yield: 1

INGREDIENTS

- 1/2 cup frozen blueberries
- whole frozen banana
- 1/2 cup almond milk
- 1/2 cup chilled water
- 1 teaspoon maca powder
- 5 ice cubes

TOPPINGS (optional)

- Chia seeds
- Maple Granola
- Kiwi fruit
- frozen blueberries
- Shredded coconut

INSTRUCTIONS

1. In a blender, place the frozen banana, frozen blueberries, almond milk, water, maca powder and ice cubes.

2. Blend until everything runs smoothly and there are no banana chunks left. The amount of time will vary depending on your blender.

3. Pour your smoothie into a bowl or large mug, add your toppings of choice and enjoy!

NOTES

Add your favourite protein powder for a post-workout meal that will keep you full for longer.

Chocolate Mousse with Vanilla cake Bowl

INGREDIENTS

- Vanilla Cake (adapted from my Vanilla Cake)
- 1/2 cup unsalted butter softened to room temperature 113g
- ½ cup canola or vegetable oil 120ml
- 1/2 cup sugar 300g
- 4 large eggs room temperature preferred
- 1 Tablespoon Nielsen-Massey Madagascar Bourbon Pure Vanilla Extract
- cups all-purpose flour 390g
- 1 Tablespoon baking powder
- 1/2 teaspoon salt
- 1 1/4 cup buttermilk room temperature preferred 300ml
- Powdered sugar for topping

Chocolate Mousse

- cup dark or semisweet chocolate chips 175g
- cups heavy cream divided (474 ml)
- 8 oz cream cheese softened (227g)
- 1 cup powdered sugar 150g
- 1 teaspoon Nielsen-Massey Madagascar Bourbon Pure Vanilla Extract
- Vanilla Bean Whipped Cream (adapted from my Homemade Whipped Cream)
- 1 1/2 cups cold heavy cream 355ml
- 1/2 cup powdered sugar 60g
- 1 ½ teaspoon Nielsen-Massey Pure Vanilla Bean Paste

Additional Toppings:

- 3 cups 400g assorted berries
- Chocolate shavings I simply used a

vegetable peeler on a chocolate bar for my chocolate shavings

INSTRUCTIONS

Vanilla Cake

- Preheat oven to 350F (175C) and prepare a jelly roll pan (12x17x1") or cookie sheet by lining the bottoms with parchment paper. Set aside.
- In the bowl of a stand mixer (or in a large bowl using an electric mixer) cream together the butter, oil and sugar, until well-combined.
- Add eggs, one at a time, beating well after each addition.
- Stir in Nielsen-Massey Pure Vanilla Extract.
- In a separate, medium-sized bowl, whisk

together flour, baking powder, and salt.

- Using a spatula and gently hand-mixing, alternate adding flour mixture and buttermilk to the butter mixture, starting and ending with flour mixture and mixing until just combined after each addition. The batter should be smooth and completely combined, but avoid over-mixing.

- Spread batter evenly into prepared jelly roll pan and bake on 350F (175C) for 18-22 minutes. When the cake is finished, the surface should spring back to the touch and a toothpick inserted in the center should come out mostly clean with few moist crumbs (no wet batter).

- Allow cakes to cool in the pan completely.

- Once cake has completely cooled, either cut into squares or use star or heart or preferred cookie cutter to cut into shapes and lightly dust with powdered sugar. Set aside until ready to serve dessert bowls.

Chocolate Mousse

- In a small saucepan, combine chocolate chips and 1/2 cup (118.5 ml) of the heavy cream over medium-low heat, stirring frequently until chocolate chips are completely melted and mixture is smooth.
- Remove from heat and pour into a heatproof bowl. Stir in Nielsen-Massey Pure Vanilla Extract.
- Allow mixture to cool completely before continuing.
- In a clean, medium-sized bowl, use an electric mixer to beat remaining 1 1/2

cups (355.5 ml) heavy cream to stiff peaks. Set aside.

- In bowl of stand mixer, combine cream cheese and (cooled) chocolate mixture, stirring until completely combined.

- Gradually add powdered sugar until completely combined. Scrape down sides of bowl as needed.

- Fold in prepared whipped cream until completely combined (don't over-mix).

- Set aside until you are ready to assemble dessert bowls (keep refrigerated in an airtight container if not assembling immediately)

Vanilla Bean Whipped Cream

- Place a medium-sized bowl (preferably

metal) in the freezer for at least 10 minutes to chill.

- Once bowl has chilled, remove from freezer and add heavy cream, powdered sugar, and Nielsen-Massey Pure Vanilla Bean Paste.
- Using an electric mixer, beat ingredients on low speed, gradually increasing speed to high, and beat on high until stiff peaks form.
- Transfer whipped cream to a piping bag fitted with a large closed-star tip.

To Assemble

- Set out the bowls that you are using for serving and evenly divide the Chocolate Mousse into each bowl, using a spoon to spread it around the bottom and up the sides to form a "nest" that covers the entire bottom of each bowl.

- Pipe your whipped cream inside the "nest" until it is completely filled

- Place powdered sugared cake cut-outs around the bowl.

- Strategically place berries around the cake cut-outs and top with chocolate shavings, if desired.

- Serve immediately.

Chocolate Banana Oatmeal Smoothie Bowl

Yield: 1 serving

INGREDIENTS

- 1/2 cup (40 g) rolled oats, gluten-free if needed
- tbsp (13 g) chia seeds
- tbsp (10 g) unsweetened cocoa powder
- 1 cup (240 ml) unsweetened almond milk**
- 1 medium-size (100 g) ripe banana, frozen

INSTRUCTIONS

- The night before, add all the ingredients except for the frozen banana to the bowl of your blender and give it a stir to ensure that everything is well combined. Cover and place in the fridge for at least 3 hours, preferably overnight. This step isn't absolutely necessary, but allowing the oats and seeds to soak for a few hours will make them easier to blend and give you a smoother, creamier smoothie.

- When ready to eat, add the frozen banana and blend on high until oats are fully broken down and a smooth and creamy consistency is reached, adding more milk if the smoothie is too thick. Transfer it to a bowl, garnish with toppings of choice, and enjoy!

NOTES

* Cook time refers to chilling time. ** You can use any non-dairy milk, or even dairy milk if you don't need this to be vegan or dairy-free. Also, if your smoothie is too thick, add a few extra splashes of milk to the blender.

Strawberry oat smoothie bowl

INGREDIENTS

- 1/4 cup rolled oats
- 1/4 cup water
- large frozen banana, sliced into chunks
- 1/2 cup Pacific Food's Organic Oat Vanilla plant-based beverage
- 1 tablespoon peanut butter
- 2 dates, pitted
- 1 heaping cup frozen strawberries
- 1/2 teaspoon vanilla extract

Toppings:

- Granola (I love my hokey pokey granola)
- Fresh berries
- Drizzle of honey/maple syrup

INSTRUCTIONS

1. Whisk together the oats with 1/4 cup water, then microwave for 1 minute, cool, then add to blender. (See tips!)

2. Place the rest of the ingredients into the blender and puree until creamy and thick. Divide into two glasses and serve!

Notes

Microwaving the oats first will help provide a smoother texture. Alternatively, you can combine the oats and water together and place in the fridge overnight before adding to the smoothie. OR, you can just add the oats raw, it will just be slightly more chewy! Not bad though- I do this all the time!

Peanut Butter, Banana and Oatmeal Smoothie Bowl With Homemade Granola And Fruit

Servings: 1 bowl

INGREDIENTS

Granola:

- 1/2 cups Bob's Red Mill Organic Old Fashioned Oats
- 1/4 cup sunflower seeds
- 1/4 cup unsweetened shredded coconut
- 1/2 tsp. cinnamon
- 1/2 tsp. kosher salt
- 1/4 cup maple syrup
- 1 Tbsp. coconut oil
- Tbsp. molasses
- 1 1/2 Tbsp. brown sugar
- 1/2 tsp. vanilla

Smoothie:

- 2 cups sliced frozen bananas
- 3 Tbsp. The Bee's Knees Peanut Butter
- 1/2 cup Bob's Red Mill Organic Old Fashioned Oats
- oz. container Greek yogurt
- 1 tsp. honey
- 1/4 - 1/2 cup milk

Toppings: sliced strawberries sliced bananas, granola

INSTRUCTIONS

1. Preheat oven to 325 degrees.
2. Line a large baking sheet with parchment paper. Set aside.
3. In medium bowl combine oats, sunflower seeds, coconut, cinnamon and salt.

4. In microwave safe bowl, combine maple syrup, coconut oil, molasses and brown sugar. Microwave mixture for one minute.

5. Add vanilla and mix until well combined.

6. Pour liquid mixture over oat mixture until all oats are thoroughly coated.

7. Spread on prepared sheet.

8. Bake for 20-25 minutes. Stirring after 10 minutes.

9. Remove from oven and let cool. Extra can be stored in airtight container.

10. Smoothie: in a blender, combine bananas, peanut butter, oats, greek yogurt, honey and 1/4 cup milk. Blend until smooth. Mixture should be thick enough to eat with a spoon. Add extra milk if you like a thinner consistency.

11. Pour the smoothie into a bowl.

12. Add toppings to taste.

Cantaloupe and Banana Smoothie Bowl

Servings 1

Ingredients

- 1 banana previously frozen
- 1/2 cantaloupe melon previously frozen
- 1 tsp flaxseeds (I used roasted ones)
- Unsweetened almond milk (or milk of your choice)

Toppings:

- 1/4 cup granola (I used a honey almond variety) or to taste
- Dried goji berries to taste

Instructions

1. Slice up a banana and half a cantaloupe melon. I suggest cutting the melon into smallish pieces so it'll be easier to blend (I used bigger chunks and it took a while to

get it all blended). Freeze in an airtight container for at least two hours, or overnight.

2. Add the banana, melon, flaxseeds, and a splash of almond milk to the blender. You may need to add more almond milk to get the blender going.

3. Pour the smoothie into a bowl and top with granola and goji berries (and/or other toppings you have on hand). Serve immediately.

Conclusion

I hope you enjoyed recreating these Buddha bowl recipes just as much as wedid creating them for you. I give our full support to you as you continue tofind more ways to nourish your body with the healthiest, tastiest, and mostsustainable foods our earth can offer.

Let this not be the end of your "Buddha bowls" journey. Always feel free torevisit your favorite recipes in this book, tweak them to your liking, and share abig bowl with family and friends. Mealtimes are always more enjoyable amonggreat company, after all.

Now, our wish for you is to have a body that is healthy, happy, and healed not just physically, but mentally, emotionally, and spiritually as well. Good luck and all the best!

Made in the USA
Coppell, TX
29 October 2020